D1717050

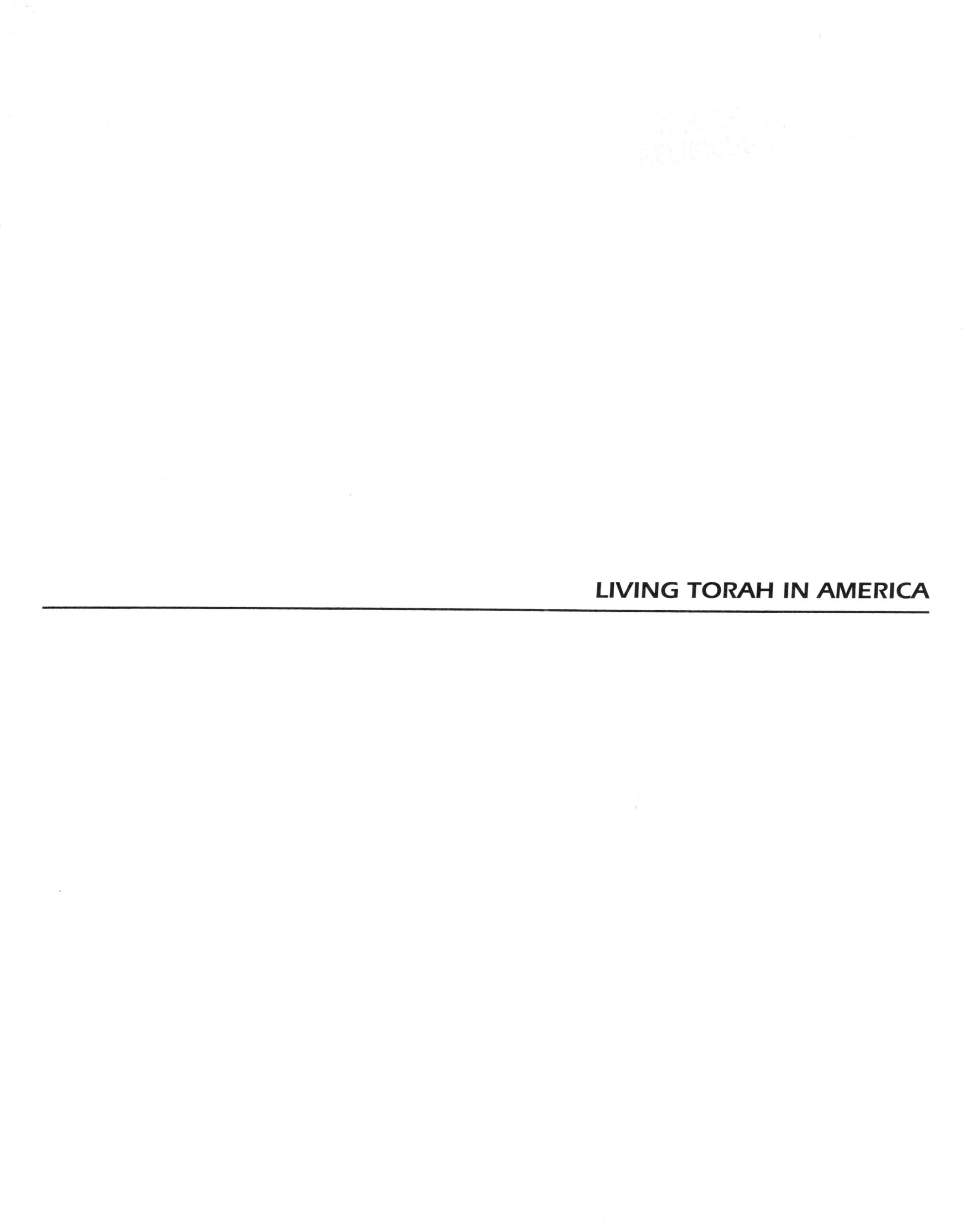

LIVING TORAH IN AMERICA

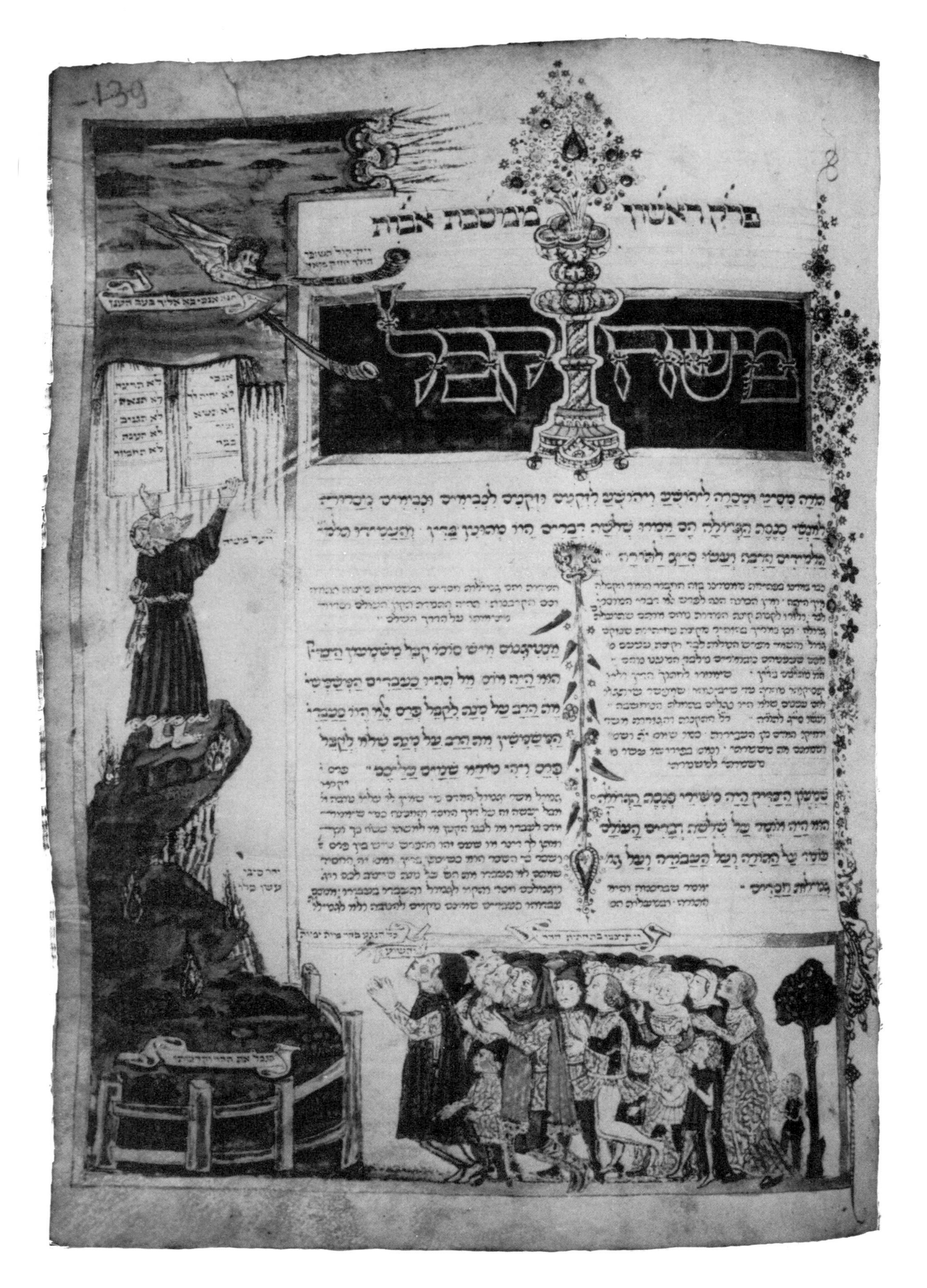

פרק ראשון ממסכת אבות

משה קבל

משה קבל תורה מסיני ומסרה ליהושע ויהושע לזקנים וזקנים לנביאים ונביאים מסרוה לאנשי כנסת הגדולה הם אמרו שלשה דברים הוו מתונים בדין והעמידו תלמידים הרבה ועשו סייג לתורה

שמעון הצדיק היה משירי כנסת הגדולה הוא היה אומר על שלשה דברים העולם עומד על התורה ועל העבודה ועל גמילות חסדים

LIVING TORAH IN AMERICA

Derekh HaTov

MAURICE LAMM

Behrman House, Inc., Publishers
West Orange, New Jersey

I dedicate this book to my grandchildren in the confidence they will all travel in *derekh hatov*:

Ellie Lamm
Michelle Lamm
Shoshana Batya Weinberg
Shira Young
Betzalel Weinberg
She'altiel Weinberg
Sholom Young
Jonathan Lamm
Gilit Weinberg
Tova Young
Lisa Lamm
Meira Young
Oriel Weinberg
Elisheva Young
Meir Shmuel Young
Perel Penina Bracha Young

Executive Editor: William Cutter
Managing Editor: Geoffrey Horn
Designer: Binns & Lubin/Martin Lubin

Library of Congress Cataloging-in-Publication Data
Lamm, Maurice.
Living Torah in America: derekh hatov/Maurice Lamm.
Includes bibliographical references and index.
ISBN 0-87441-513-6
1. Jewish way of life–Juvenile literature. 2. Orthodox Judaism–Customs and practices–Juvenile literature. [1. Orthodox Judaism. 2. Judaism–Customs and practices.] I. Title.
BM723.L26 1991
296.7'4–dc20 91-15178
CIP
AC

Behrman House, Inc., Publishers
235 Watchung Avenue
West Orange, NJ 07052

CONTENTS

ACKNOWLEDGMENTS

I am grateful to many people for bringing this work to fruition. Jacob Behrman, the publisher, blends a shrewd entrepreneurial spirit with uncompromising taste and a personal mission to contribute creatively to Jewish society. My colleague and editor, Rabbi William Cutter, is everything a writer needs: a good friend, an enthusiastic supporter, a talented midwife, a discreet *nudge*, and a sophisticated intellectual. Seymour Rossel, who helped lay the groundwork for this project, offered a clarity of communication with young people that was indispensable. As managing editor, Geoffrey Horn brought tact and sophistication to the task of supervising the transition from manuscript to finished book. My wife, Shirley, gave me her usual wise counsel through the many *gilgulim* of the manuscript. Rabbi Simcha Fishbane of Israel did commendable research in new pedagogic areas; Stacy Laveson and Nancy Kasten Also provided significant research assistance. My colleague Rabbi Daniel Landes helped through his creative reading of the material in process. My distinguished colleague Rabbi Hershel Schachter, head of the Adina and Marcus Katz Kollel at Yeshiva University, reviewed the many halakhic components and, as usual, offered trenchant and valuable criticism.

MAURICE LAMM

Palm Springs, CA

INTRODUCTION

I embarked on this work for young people because I realize the value the sages placed on *girsa de' yankusa*, "learning absorbed by the very young," which the Talmud considers the "best saved," the longest remembered. In youth, values and attitudes are deeply implanted, and education is at its most effective.

The phrase that most intruded itself into my mind during the writing and editing of this book is "The Torah is out of this world." I understand this often quoted and widely accepted phrase in both its positive and negative senses. Positively, it bespeaks a wonderment for that magnificent document which comes from HaShem and has served as a constant guide for the individual throughout the record of civilized existence. Negatively, it is a way of saying that much of the Torah is unrealizable idealism; that by its nature Torah is beyond human accomplishment, to be studied only for its intrinsic value; and that we pay reverence to the Torah for its awesome, "beyond-this-world" quality.

Yet the Torah is not beyond this world. Torah itself proclaims this, saying of itself, *Lo va'shamayim ḥi*, "It is not in heaven." That is what I try to demonstrate here. In order to do this, I seek to implant the observance of the mitzvot directly into the flesh of daily life—no more, no less. Can it be that dressing in the morning is not merely a single-minded activity aimed at "looking good" but also contains an idealistic, even a Jewish, component? Can it be that getting out of bed has more significance than just making sure we are not late in beginning our daily routine?

I spent a night at one of my children's homes and awakened at six in the morning. The house was quiet. But in the bathroom, silent and alone with the door ajar, was my five-year-old granddaughter standing on a little stool near the sink. With one hand she was rubbing her eyes; with the other she was holding a washing pitcher. "Good morning," I said. "Good morning," she mumbled. "I have to take six." What she meant was that she had to wash each hand three times alternately, just as observant Jews have been washing their hands ritually upon arising every morning for more than 2,000 years.

Now this practice does not express a stunning theological belief or a profound moral insight. It is simply a behavior—a behavior that points you toward **derekh hatov** (דֶּרֶךְ הַטּוֹב), the path of goodness. Performing this practice makes you a better Jew. It connects you to the Jewish past and brings the Torah back into this world, even as it helps to ensure the survival of our people.

I believe the machinery of survival is fueled by behavior. It is the premise of **halakhah** (הֲלָכָה), the body of Jewish law, and it is the premise of this work.

For this reason, I based this book on the order found in the classic code of Jewish religious behavior, the **Shulḥan Arukh** (שֻׁלְחָן עָרוּךְ, "Prepared Table"), the sixteenth-century code by Rabbi Joseph Karo. The Shulḥan Arukh has served as the daily guide for Jews for more than 400 years, and it can serve us today. I have tried to clothe the bare halakhot with ethical applications in a contemporary style. Books on ethics are usually separated from those on religious behavior. Here I have made a shy attempt at blending the Shulḥan Arukh with the spirit of the well-known Jewish ethical treatise **Mesillat Yesharim** (מְסִלַּת יְשָׁרִים, "The Pathway of the Righteous").

I know that teachers of religion, whether parents or pedagogues, are deeply sensitive to the significance of *girsa de' yankusa.* I hope that our partnership will succeed—for HaShem's sake and for the good of the next generation.

LIVING TORAH IN AMERICA

כֹּה אָמַר ה׳
עִמְדוּ עַל־דְּרָכִים וּרְאוּ
וְשַׁאֲלוּ לִנְתִבוֹת עוֹלָם
אֵי־זֶה דֶרֶךְ הַטּוֹב וּלְכוּ־בָהּ
וּמִצְאוּ מַרְגּוֹעַ לְנַפְשְׁכֶם׃

Thus said the Lord:
Stand by the roads and consider,
Inquire about ancient paths:
Which is the way of goodness?
Travel it, and find tranquillity for your souls.
(Jeremiah 6:16)

PROLOGUE

THE FULL-TIME JEW

This book is about the weekdays in the life of a Jew, not Sabbaths or holidays or once-in-a-lifetime celebrations. Its locus is not the synagogue but the home and the school, the office and the market. In short, this book seeks to expand the horizons of the many Jews who locate Judaism only in the synagogue on special days. It says that being truly Jewish means being a full-time Jew.

FULL-TIME OR PART-TIME?

How can you tell whether you are a part-time or a full-time Jew? And why does it make a difference?

If you only keep Shabbat, you are no more than a part-time Jew.

If you are Jewish on the High Holy Days, but that's all—you may be a nice person, but you are only a part-time Jew.

If you keep the mitzvot between HaShem and man, but you don't act decently toward other human beings, you are not a full-time Jew.

If you are a nice person, but you don't keep the mitzvot, you are not a full-time Jew.

A Jew should not act like a Jew only at special times, such as a bar mitzvah or Shabbat morning or Pesaḥ. That is being only a part-time Jew.

The full-time Jew recognizes that HaShem created weekdays as well as special days. The full-time Jew understands that HaShem wants us to acknowledge Him every day as the Creator of all time.

The full-time Jew knows that you cannot take a vacation from HaShem. You may travel to London to see the queen, but HaShem, the King of Kings, doesn't go on vacation—ever.

The full-time Jew recognizes that if you are nice to only some of the people only some of the time, you are not a believer in a Creator for all time.

WHY PART-TIME DOESN'T WORK

The problem with part-time is that it just doesn't work. You cannot be a part-time mother or a part-time daughter. Your father cannot be

Since the sixteenth century, the Shulḥan Arukh has been a daily guide for the full-time Jew.

a part-time provider or teacher or friend. Some things cannot be done properly unless they're done full-time.

A part-time worker doesn't commit himself totally to the job. A part-time doctor can't be a fully effective healer.

To be successful in your Jewishness, you need to do it full-time. That is what HaShem wants from you: Be a full-time Jew.

HOW YOU CAN BE A FULL-TIME JEW

This book shows how every week in the life of a Jew can be a "good week," **shavu'a tov** (שָׁבוּעַ טוֹב). It says, over and over again, that you must be mindful of HaShem—every day, in a Jewish way.

Now this does not mean you have to study Torah hour after hour or daven all day long, or that you need to do kind things for people every waking minute. Relax.

What being a full-time Jew does mean is that we must be conscious of HaShem by doing what He asks us to do, whenever He asks us to do it.

We expect that when we become full-time Jews, we will merit a full-time God, one who protects us and provides for us—all day, every day.

CHAPTER ONE

A NEW DAY

שִׁוִּתִי יהוה לְנֶגְדִּי תָמִיד.

I put God always before me.
(Ps. 16:8)

You are now a young adult. This is a very special time in your life, a time when many changes take place in you. Some changes are physical—these are easy for you to recognize. Other changes involve the way you see, hear, feel, and think about the world around you.

Up to now, many things about your Judaism may have seemed somewhat confusing. You have learned bits of Judaism at one age level, pieces of it at another. You have experienced Jewishness as it was taught to you by your parents and grandparents and by a variety of teachers. Under these circumstances it is difficult to have a coherent understanding of Judaism. But now you are old enough to begin to make sense of what it means to be a Jew. It is time to take the narratives in the Torah and legends in the Midrash, together with the mitzvot and the values they suggest, and put them in some kind of order. There are things about being Jewish that you are now ready to understand and take to heart.

Many years ago, God made a covenant, a sort of contract, with our ancestors. This is the covenant on which bar or bat mitzvah is based. To enter this covenant means that you must walk in God's ways and follow the instructions of Torah. You already know this is not as simple as it sounds. And we have an example here before us, immediately, as we begin this book. What word do we use in English to refer to God?

SACRED NAMES

There are seven proper names for God in Hebrew. They are all sacred and may never be erased or defaced.

For years and years, Jews have avoided spelling out the name of God—not in books, not in magazines, not even in English. There is a long tradition behind this avoidance. The name of God has been considered too holy to place on paper or in a book. We cherish God too deeply to swear by His name, to use it casually, even to use it sincerely except on special occasions. The Talmud says: "Every place where the unnecessary mention of the Divine Name is found, there

All over the world, young Jews willingly take on *ol hamitzvot*, the yoke of the commandments. Left, a bar mitzvah in Paris; below, students in Los Angeles give thanks for a refreshed soul by davening Shaḥarit.

A Note on Sources

To help you learn more about Judaism, we have followed current scholarly practice in citing sources quoted in the text. You can find a complete list of sources and a key to abbreviations at the back of this book. A table in Chapter 6 lists all the books of the Hebrew Bible, giving their names in Hebrew as well as English.

poverty will be found" (Ned. 7b). Even in the Torah itself, and in the siddur, God is referred to by a code word of four Hebrew letters which combines all the tenses—*was*, *is*, and *will be*—to mean eternal or everlasting God. When books containing God's name grow old and worn, they must not be destroyed. Instead, we bury them, even as we bury a human being.

What does the use of this special Hebrew name reveal? A great deal! It is proof that we are in awe of God, even as we love God. It is proof that God is close to us, even as God is beyond our power and understanding. God controls the whole universe, yet He also concerns Himself with our personal destiny. He is so close that we call Him by many names, as we would someone we truly love.

What about names for God in everyday languages, such as English? In his commentary on the Shulḥan Arukh, the seventeenth-century rabbi Shabbetai ben Meir HaKohen observes that in everyday languages the names used for God are most often based on adjectives, or attributes rather than proper nouns (ShaKh, Yoreh De'ah, 179:11). English terms such as "Almighty" or "Compassionate" name God by describing His qualities. Unlike God's seven proper Hebrew names, these English names may be erased. Nevertheless, the Geonim—rabbinic scholars of eighth-century Babylonia—cautioned that all books which specifically refer to God, even by names based on adjectives, must be treated with special respect.

What guidance should we follow in referring to God in English? On the one hand, since "God" is an English word and not one of the sacred Hebrew names, we should be able to use it freely. On the other hand, since "God" in English is a proper noun and not an attribute name, we run the risk of violating the warning against using God's name needlessly, as the Geonim cautioned. Even if we agree that printing God's name in a book that teaches about Judaism should not be considered "needless use," there is still another problem. Many centuries ago, books were works of art, individually decorated in silver and gold, and treasured by their owners. Today, books are produced in large quantities by machine, and we do not handle them as gently or respectfully as we should. So even in a book that teaches Torah, we need to be very careful in deciding how to refer to God.

QUESTIONS OF AUTHORITY

In this book, therefore, I will primarily use **HaShem** when writing about God. I will use the word "God" only when quoting from the Bible and when it occurs in a berakhah, so that students do not learn the wrong way of pronouncing the blessing.

In Hebrew, הַשֵּׁם literally means "the name." For those of us who seek to follow the ways of Torah, this custom of using HaShem when writing in English is not a very old practice. There is no reference in the Torah to the use of HaShem for this purpose. This use of HaShem began because our people needed a way to refer to God in everyday language without actually pronouncing the sacred Name. So, for example, when they wanted to thank God, they said, *barukh HaShem*, "Praise to God."

By using the name HaShem, I am telling you that I not only love HaShem but also respect Him; He is close to me, yet at the same time beyond my power and comprehension. Although the Torah does not tell us what word to use when we write about HaShem in English, I have turned to the Talmud and its commentaries, to the Shulḥan Arukh and its commentaries, and finally to the tradition as Jews have observed it from the time of the Shulḥan Arukh to our own day.

Now this brings up a vital question: What sources of authority can answer the many questions I have about Judaism? I am a rabbi with many years of experience. But what happens when I find a question to which I do not know the answer? Where does a rabbi turn?

The rabbi does exactly what other Jews must try to do—go back to the resources of our faith. I look in Torah and try to find the general answer there. I look in Talmud and try to find greater clarification. Then I look in the Shulḥan Arukh and try to find the answer there. For a final, definitive answer, I can look to all those great scholars who have interpreted the Shulḥan Arukh and applied it to the problems of their own times.

Worn-out prayer books, tefillin, tallitot, and other sacred objects are not just thrown away. They must be buried in a Jewish cemetery with honor and respect—according to custom, near the grave of a Jewish scholar.

Major Halakhic Authorities

THE RIF: The *Hilkhot Rav Alfas*, commonly called the Rif, an acronym for the author's name, **R**abbi **I**saac al-**F**asi (1013-1103). The Rif is the preeminent authority in Spain and North Africa. It came to be known as the **Talmud Katan** (תַּלְמוּד קָטָן), or "abbreviated Talmud." The Rif follows the order of the Talmud and decides outstanding questions of law between the close of the Talmudic period and the eleventh century.

THE RAMBAM: Maimonides (1135-1204) is usually known as **Rambam**, an acronym based on the name **R**abbi **M**oshe **b**en **M**aimon. Rambam was one of the greatest scholars in Jewish history. Although he wrote works of philosophy and science, as well as commentaries on Bible and Mishnah, he is most famous for his law code, the **Mishneh Torah** (מִשְׁנֵה תּוֹרָה). The code, which covers fourteen volumes, is sometimes called the **Yad HaḤazakah**, which literally means "the mighty hand"; the name arose because in Hebrew יָד is made of י and ד, which together add up to fourteen. The Mishneh Torah does not follow the order of the Talmud but instead organizes the laws and principles of Judaism according to the internal logic of the halakhah.

THE TUR: The four Turim, or "rows," by Rabbi Jacob ben Rabbenu Asher (1270?-1340), form the basis for the Shulḥan Arukh. Written in Germany, about 150 years after the Mishneh Torah and 200 years before the Shulḥan Arukh, the Tur describes Jewish practice from morning to night, from weekdays to holidays. Unlike Rambam's code, which covers all of Judaism, the Tur presents only laws relevant to daily Jewish living.

THE SHULḤAN ARUKH: The Shulḥan Arukh, which means "Prepared Table," is based directly on the Tur and was written by Rabbi Joseph Karo (1488-1575) in the sixteenth century in Eretz Yisrael. Karo had a brilliant mind, and his code remains today the most authoritative source of all Jewish law. The code has four divisions:

1. Oraḥ Ḥayyim ("The Way of Life"): Considering the Torah as the source of everyday living, this division describes Jewish conduct in daily life, Shabbat, and festivals.

2. Yoreh De'ah ("Teaching Knowledge"): This section teaches traditions and laws that require rulings by authorities, such as kashrut, mikveh, brit milah, and mourning. Rabbis today must know this volume and its sources in order to qualify as authorities.

3. Even HaEzer ("The Rock of Help"): This division, whose title is based on the Bible's use of the term "helpmate" to describe woman, deals with male-female relations and with families. It covers the laws of marriage and divorce.

4. Ḥoshen Mishpat ("The Breastplate of Judgment"): The laws of Judaism cover not only religious practices but also civil and criminal disputes. Ḥoshen Mishpat—named for the breastplate which the ancient High Priest, or **kohen** (כֹּהֵן), wore and consulted regarding political affairs affecting the entire nation—covers laws of evidence, judges, personal injury cases, and other legal matters.

THE REMA: Moses Isserles (1525?-1572), a Polish rabbi known as the Rema, is famous chiefly for his additions, or "glosses," to the Shulḥan Arukh. His additions are called the **Mapah** ("Tablecloth") to Karo's "Prepared Table." While Karo wrote mainly for Sephardic Jewry—the Jewish communities of North Africa and the Middle East—the Rema wrote his glosses for the Ashkenazic communities of Germany and Eastern Europe.

LATER CODES: The following works apply the laws of the Shulḥan Arukh to problems of their own times and include customs introduced in a variety of lands.

1. Shulḥan Arukh HaRav, by the founder of Ḥabad Lubavitch Ḥasidism, Rabbi Shneur Zalman of Lyady (1747-1813).

2. Ḥayyei Adam, by Rabbi Abraham Danzig (1748-1820).

3. Kitzur Shulḥan Arukh, a condensation of the original work by Rabbi Solomon Ganzfried (1804-1866). Written in a simple—but sometimes oversimplified—style, this text is found in many Jewish households.

4. Arukh HaShulḥan, written by Rabbi Yeḥiel Michael Epstein (1829-1908) of Novogrudok, covers all four books of the original Shulḥan Arukh. A comprehensive work renowned among rabbinic scholars, Arukh HaShulḥan includes all halakhic decisions down to Epstein's own day.

5. Mishnah Berurah, by the saintly Ḥafetz Ḥayyim, Rabbi Israel Meir HaKohen Kagan (1838-1933) of Radin, Poland. This work, a detailed commentary on the Oraḥ Ḥayyim section of the Shulḥan Arukh, is a scholarly, authoritative work of contemporary Jewish law. It is one of the most important sources of guidance for observant Jews.

(טז) קדושת כתר. פי' במקום שאנו אומרים נקדש במוסף אומרים במקצת מדינות כתר יתנו לך וכו' וכתב ב"י הטעם דאין נכון להיות באותה שעה כתר דתפילין עליו כדאיתא בפס הזוהר מביאו ב"י לענין הפילין בח"מ בסי' ל"ח. ותמהני על מ"ב רמ"א שהמנהג לסלקם בר"ח והלא בח"מ אמור עפי לענין תפילין שלא להניחם כמו שהארדע"ז ב"י בשם הזוהר ולפי"ה מניחין תפילין במדינות אלו ואפי' בברכה ואלו באמצעות קדושת כתר שיש במדינות אחרות נאמר תפילין והדרנא (°) בברכה דוכתי שאין מניחין תפילין מ"מ אין חולצין אם היו עליו כבר (°) וכאן נימא [illegible] ... כיון שאין כתר ע"כ נראה דהמנהג כן שאינו חולצן אין עליו תלונה על שהוא סותר המנהג כי יש לו על מי לסמוך:

כז (א) בזרוע שמאל. דכתיב ידכה פי' יד (°) כהה ... שסמאל ... (ב) הקובד"ו. בל"א עלינבוגי"ן ויליף מדכתיב והי' לך לאות

הגה **לא** וה"ה במוצאי [illegible] במקום שאומרים במוסף **(טז)** (כג) קדושת **לב** כתר. תיכו נוהגים לסלקם קודם מוסף בכל מקום [ב"י]:

כו דין מי שאין לו אלא תפלה אחת. ובו ב' סעיפים:

א א *אם אין לו אלא תפלה אחת מניח אותה שיש לו ומברך עליה שכל אחת מצוה בפני עצמה ג והוא הדין אם יש לו שתיהם ג ויש לו **א** (א) שום אונס שאינו יכול להניח אלא אחת מניח אותה שיכול:

ב ד אם אינו מניח אלא של ראש לבד מברך עליה על מצות תפילין לבד: הגה ונדידן דנוהגים לברך בכל יום ב' ברכות יברך על של ראש גם כן שתי ברכות ואם הניח של יד לבד מברך להניח לבד [טור]:

כז מקום הנחתן ואופן הנחתן. ובו יא סעיפים:

א א *מקום הנחתן של יד (א) בזרוע (א) שמאל בבשר התופח שבעצם ג שבין (ב) **א** (ג) הקובד"ו ובית השחי ג ויטה התפלה מעט לצד הגוף בענין שכשיכוף זרועו למטה יהיו כנגד לבו ונמצא מקיים והיו הדברים האלה על לבבך: הגה וצריך להניח **ב** נראה הבלט הסמוך (ג) להקובד"ו אבל לא כחצי העלם הסמוך כבתי [סמ"ק] ו [נידם שאין לו יד (ד) רק זרוע יניח בלא ברכה] [תוספות פ' הקומץ כתבו דגידם חייב ובה"ז כתב דפטור]:

ב ד המנהג הנכון שיהא היו"ד של קשר תפלה של יד לצד הלב ☞ והתפלה עליו לצד חוץ * יש ליזהר שלא תזוז (ה) יוד של הקשר מהתפלה: המנהג

לא וה"ה בח"ה. ועט' ל"ח ד"ח שלא להניחם. כלל לינו אלא מנהג לאלים: בח"ה והזוהר מחמיר מאד בדבר לכן כתב הרמ"ע בתשובה לחלוץ קודם הלל והם ל (°) אחר הלל וכ"כ הלבוש סי' ל"ח וכן ראוי לנהוג ועי' סי' תרל"ח ס"ז בהג"ה: וג"ל כח"ה בל סוכות אף הב"ן יחלוץ קודם הלל בעוד שמוכרין ההתגון: **לב** כתר יתנו לך. כן מנהג הספרדיים ולכן אין ראוי להיות כתר של תפ לין עליו:

כו א שום אונס. כגון שצריך לצאת לדרך ואין יכול לעכב להניח ש"י מניח ש"ר לבד ולא חיישינן למ"ש כל זמן שבין עיניך יהיו שתים (הרא"ב) וקשה מנ"ל הא דלמא דוקא באונס גמור כגון שיש לו מכה ביד הבל מבוס איחור דרכו לא התירו לו לבטל מצות תפילין וי"ל דמ"מ יניחם הש"ב אלא דקמ"ל דאע"ג דאין יכול להניח (°) עתה ש"י מ"מ יניח ש"ר לבד ועמ"ש סי' ל"ח ס"ט:

כז א הקובד"ו. בל"א עלינבוגי"ן: ב כראה העלם. פי' (°) בחצי העלם ובבד"ה כ' ואין לסמוך ע"ז להכשיר להניח בכל חצי הזרוע כ"א בבשר התופח כלשון הרמב"ם והטור ובלשון הגמרא או קיבורת עכ"ל ☞ ול"ע (°) למה כתבו בס"ז לכן כ"ל דתף בסמ"ק כוונתו שיתנה דוקא בבשר התופח אלא שבא למעט שלא להניחו באמצע בחצי בלשי בית השחי שהוא

נ"כ תופה: נ גידם. ז"ל ד"מ בא"ז כתב גידם פטור אף על פי שנשאר לו זרוע להניח שם אבל בתו' סוף פ' הקומץ דף ל ז משמע דהלכ' כמ"ד חייב אם

באר הגולה

א תוספות ... שם ... ב ... רש"י ... ג ... ה ...

עטרת זקנים

נתיב חיים

הגהות רעק"א

חתם סופר

באר היטב

שערי תשובה

ביאור הגר"א

יד אפרים

לבושי שרד

אשל אברהם

חכמת שלמה

מחצית השקל

פמ"ג

1A
1B
2
3
4
5
6
7
8

A Page of Shulḥan Arukh

1A SHULḤAN ARUKH, the basic text by Rabbi Joseph Karo (1488-1575).

1B MAPAH, commentary by the Rema, Rabbi Moses Isserles (1525?-1572).

2 MAGEN DAVID, discussions of halakhic problems in the Talmud, Tur, and Shulḥan Arukh by a Polish rabbi, David ben Shmuel HaLevi (1586-1667), known as the Taz.

3 MAGEN AVRAHAM, a highly concise commentary on the Shulḥan Arukh by another Polish rabbi, Avraham Evli Gumbiner (1637?-1683).

4 MAḤATZIT HASHEKEL, by Rabbi Shmuel HaLevi (1720-1806) of Kolin, Bohemia—an explanation of the Magen Avraham.

5 BE'ER HETEV, a more basic commentary by Rabbi Yehuda ben Shimon Ashkenazi of Tiktin, Poland.

6 BE'ER HAGOLA, by Moshe Rivkis, a Polish rabbi of the mid-seventeenth century known as HeḤasid ("The Pious").

7 SHA'AREI TESHUVAH, by Ḥayyim Mordecai Margolis, Rav of Dubnow, Poland. This commentary, written more than 200 years after the Shulḥan Arukh, sums up halakhic rulings from the responsa literature in the intervening period.

8 BE'UR HAGRA, difficult, scholarly commentary by Rabbi Elijah ben Solomon Żalman, the Vilna Gaon (1720-1797).

THE SHULḤAN ARUKH

Moses received Torah on Mount Sinai and handed it down to Joshua. Joshua handed Torah down to the elders. The elders handed it down to the prophets. And the prophets passed it down to the Men of the Great Assembly. In time, the oral law interpreting the written law was also written down, and this became the Talmud. Many more commentaries were written—on Torah and on Talmud—and these were handed down through the generations.

Moses Maimonides—the Rambam—wrote a code of law, and so did other great rabbis, such as Isaac al-Fasi, called the Rif. Joseph Karo wrote the code of law known as the Shulḥan Arukh, and it became a standard to be passed down from generation to generation. The Shulḥan Arukh and its commentators are the main authority for this book.

The Shulḥan Arukh tells us many things. It tells us what to eat and how to dress, what is work and what is prayer, what we should and should not do on Shabbat and the festivals. Still, we must always remember that the Shulḥan Arukh does not have answers to all the questions that come up in every era. We must look at a wide range of authoritative writings before we can confidently make decisions about how we should live our lives according to the traditions, beliefs, and values of Judaism.

Like other rabbis, I have for many years studied Torah and Talmud and the halakhah as it is found in the Shulḥan Arukh. I have been fortunate enough to sit at the feet of great teachers: my grandfather, Rabbi Yehoshua Baumol, and my renowned rebbe, Rabbi Joseph Soloveitchik. I have learned from many rabbis, living and dead, and I will try to pass on to you some of what I have learned about walking in the ways of HaShem. I write this book with faith that HaShem will guide me and give me the insights to teach His Torah.

Rabbi Joseph Soloveitchik, a renowned rebbe, teacher, and scholar, guided thousands of American rabbis to a deeper understanding of faith and halakhah.

THE RIGHT WAY TO OPEN YOUR EYES

If you were thinking Jewishly, and preparing to write a code of laws for Jews to follow, you might begin with rules for what to do when the sun goes down, because that is when the Jewish day actually begins. And, certainly, that is one way a code of Jewish law could be written.

But that is not how the Shulḥan Arukh begins. It begins with the morning. Morning is a time we give to many little things—washing up, brushing our teeth, getting dressed, and so on. And when we are concerned with the smaller things in life, we tend to forget the really important things.

So the Shulḥan Arukh (in Hebrew, שֻׁלְחָן עָרוּךְ literally means a "prepared" or "set" table) begins with a menu of ways we can remember the important things, even as we are doing things that seem trifling and small. By showing us at the very beginning how even the little things we do can reflect our most important principles, the Shulḥan Arukh helps us live up to the great ideals we set for ourselves.

The Shulḥan Arukh begins with the right way to open your eyes. The first words in its first chapter are:

שִׁוִּיתִי ה׳ לְנֶגְדִּי תָמִיד.

I put HaShem always before me.

Why begin here? For one thing, the Shulḥan Arukh is a book of Jewish law, and Jewish law itself begins in the Torah. Torah is the word of HaShem. So the way we behave has everything to do with the way we think about HaShem. To "put HaShem always before you" means to keep in mind, at all times, that HaShem is near.

SOMEONE IS ALWAYS WATCHING

How can thinking that HaShem is near change your behavior? The answer is obvious. You behave very differently when you think no one important is watching you than when you know someone important is watching. Jewish tradition says that someone important is *always* watching.

An old story illustrates the point. A rabbi was walking along the road when a man driving a cart stopped to pick him up. They drove a short way until the driver brought the cart to a halt. "Look," he said, "there's a nice orchard with many apples on the trees. Surely no one will notice if I take one for me and one for my horse. You keep an eye out, and if anyone comes, yell 'Someone is looking!' and I will hurry back to the cart."

As the driver approached the gate to the orchard, suddenly the rabbi yelled out, "Someone is looking!" The driver ran back to the cart, hurriedly got in, and drove the horse and cart away in a flash.

They had not gone very far when the driver again stopped. "Look," he said, "there's a barn full of oats, and so close to the road. I will just get a few oats for my horse. No one will miss a few oats. But if anyone comes along, yell out and warn me."

Just as the driver reached the barn door, the rabbi yelled out, "Someone is looking!" With a jump and a bound, the driver was back on the cart and ready to drive off. But this time, the driver paused to look around. "There is no one coming at all!" he said to the rabbi. "Why did you yell out, 'Someone is looking'?"

The rabbi glanced upward, then smiled at the driver and winked. "Someone is *always* looking," he said.

We consult the Mishneh Torah, responsa, and other books to answer our questions about Jewish traditions, values, and beliefs.

ARISE LIKE A LION

Imagine: The alarm clock rings. You turn over and look at the time. Now you have to make a choice. Should you get up and start your day, or should you turn over and go back to sleep for just a few more minutes?

You might wonder how a small decision like this one could possibly be relevant to a discussion dealing with an issue as important as our relationship with HaShem. But as we will see, even something as apparently minor as getting out of bed in the morning can reflect a deeper attitude about ourselves and our approach to leading a Jewish life. We read in the Shulḥan Arukh that HaShem wants each of us to "arise like a lion." The Shulḥan Arukh knows how tempting it is for you to go back to sleep in the morning. It knows that a little urge we all have inside us makes us want to stay in bed.

What the Shulḥan Arukh means when it tells you to "arise like a lion" is that you must get up energetically to face the new day. For a Jew, rising up vigorously from sleep borders on a mitzvah. Every day of our lives we try to do what HaShem wants: we serve HaShem with all our hearts, all our souls, and all our might. If we were serving a human king or queen in this way, we would get up as soon as we were called. But we are serving HaShem, and that makes getting up—and exercising our bodies and our minds—even more urgent. Arising with energy is the first test each morning, the first chance we have to show our respect and devotion to HaShem.

You may say, "Get right out of bed? That's too much for me!" Believe it or not, people have been saying just that for hundreds and hundreds of years. So Judaism has an answer. It may be hard to do the first time. It may be hard to do the second time. But if you keep at it, after four or five times, rising immediately will seem as natural as can be. As the Talmud says, "If you make the effort to do the right thing, HaShem helps" (Yoma 38b).

Physical exercise borders on a mitzvah.

WASHING UP

Now you are out of bed. And you got up not just because you wanted to, but because it was the right thing to do. So what's next? Washing up.

Science teaches us that much disease comes from the bacteria that naturally gather on our bodies. Washing with soap keeps bacteria from breeding and infecting us and making us ill. Similarly, plaque naturally collects on our teeth. If left unchecked, plaque will cake on the teeth, causing decay, cavities, and toothaches. Brushing and flossing teeth removes the plaque and keeps our teeth healthy.

Of course, cleaning our bodies and brushing our teeth are healthful. What is amazing is that the Jewish code of law knew this long before modern science proved that dirt can cause illness. In fact, halakhah spells out the times when washing is absolutely required: after rising from sleep, before leaving the rest room, after cutting fingernails or toenails, after touching our shoes, before eating, before praying, and so on. But precisely because we wash our hands to fulfill HaShem's command—and not just to keep healthy—we must do it in a particular way. This regular washing reminds us of the way the kohanim washed their hands in the days of the ancient Temple, to prepare for a day filled with holy activities. You, too, are preparing for a day of significant activities. You wash your hands in preparation for your day the same way they did, by pouring water from a cup alternately over each hand three times. This washing is accompanied by a blessing, or berakhah, which is recited outside the washroom:

By developing our bodies as well as our minds, we show respect and devotion to HaShem, who created us in His image.

בָּרוּךְ אַתָּה, יהוה אֱלֹהֵינוּ, מֶלֶךְ הָעוֹלָם, אֲשֶׁר קִדְּשָׁנוּ בְּמִצְוֹתָיו וְצִוָּנוּ
עַל נְטִילַת יָדָיִם.

Blessed are You, Lord, our God, King of the universe, who has sanctified us through His commandments and has commanded us about washing the hands.

Saying the berakhah makes it clear that we are performing this action for HaShem.

There is a real difference between doing things for a "logical" reason and doing them for HaShem. The difference is not seen from the outside; it is something you feel on the inside. When you come in from playing football, you stop to wash your hands to make them clean. That is a logical thing to do. But when you wash your hands in a prescribed ceremonial way, even if you have just come fresh from a shower, you are not doing it because it is logical—you are doing it because Jewish law requires it.

What is logical for one person may not be logical for another. Individual needs change, environments differ, and circumstances evolve, so that what seems logical today may be considered nonsensical tomorrow, let alone 200 years from now. But HaShem is an unchanging, all-wise Father. He is the Power who created us and who knows our needs. Following HaShem's laws, rather than our personal preferences, enables us, our ancestors, and our descendants to trust and believe in the same God. It fortifies the Jewish people to survive with integrity intact.

Good Morning!

Here is what to do when you first wake up in the morning.

1. Thank HaShem. Before getting out of bed, recite in either Hebrew or English:

מוֹדֶה אֲנִי לְפָנֶיךָ מֶלֶךְ חַי וְקַיָּם שֶׁהֶחֱזַרְתָּ בִּי נִשְׁמָתִי בְּחֶמְלָה, רַבָּה אֱמוּנָתֶךָ.

I gratefully thank You, O living and eternal King, for you have returned my faculties [soul] within me with compassion. Your faithfulness is generous.

2. Get up right away—like a lion—to face the new day.

3. Go directly to the washroom and wash, both to be clean and to emulate the ancient kohen before he began the Temple service. From a washing cup or pitcher—using your own energy, not from the faucet—pour water three times alternately over each hand up to the wrist, as follows: right, left; right, left; right, left. Now wash your eyes and face—to be clean, but primarily to attend to the image of HaShem in which you were created.

4. Recite in Hebrew or English the blessing over washing the hands:

בָּרוּךְ אַתָּה, יהוה אֱלֹהֵינוּ, מֶלֶךְ הָעוֹלָם, אֲשֶׁר קִדְּשָׁנוּ בְּמִצְוֹתָיו וְצִוָּנוּ
עַל נְטִילַת יָדָיִם.

Blessed are You, Lord, our God, King of the universe, who has sanctified us through His commandments and has commanded us about washing the hands.

Young Jews in Jerusalem collecting photos of eminent rebbes. "The wise shall obtain honor" (Prov. 3:35).

IN HIS IMAGE

A famous story about Hillel shows why HaShem wants us to keep our bodies clean. Once, after a lesson with his students, the great teacher started to hurry away. The students rushed after him. "Where are you going in such a hurry?" they wanted to know.

"I am going to the bathhouse to wash myself," said Hillel.

"But why in such a rush?" they asked.

Hillel answered, "Imagine that the king decides to have a statue made—a statue that looks just like him. The statue is set up in the square outside the palace gate. One day the king decides to go to look at the statue. The palace guards hear that the king is coming and rush to make the statue clean. After all, the king would be upset to see that his people did not care enough about him to keep his statue clean.

"It is the same way with our bodies," said Hillel. "The Torah says that HaShem made us in His image. So our bodies are like the statue. HaShem is not pleased when we forget to keep ourselves clean. And that is why I am rushing to the bathhouse."

THE FIRST COMMANDMENT

Directions about getting up early, washing hands, and taking good care of ourselves—these may seem like a lot of details for a code of Jewish law to bother about. They seem to be among the smaller things in life. None of them, for example, is specifically mentioned in the Written Torah, and certainly not in the Ten Commandments.

Indirectly, however, all these things are included in the Ten Commandments. If you remember the first rule—"I put HaShem always before me"—you will see that these rules are a way of putting the First Commandment ("I am HaShem, your God") into action. They remind us that we were created in the image of HaShem and must treat ourselves accordingly.

In the succeeding chapters, we will have many opportunities to examine the varied ways we put HaShem before us throughout the day—whether we are at school or at home, alone or with our family. By putting HaShem before us, we find derekh hatov and follow the pathways to Jewish religious life.

CHAPTER TWO

GETTING DRESSED

זֶה אֵלִי וְאַנְוֵהוּ.

This is my God and I shall glorify Him.

(Ex. 15:2)

The way you dress sets you apart from other people as surely as the way you think. Nearly every tribe, clan, sect, group, faction, school, and clique wears some special items of clothing to identify itself and to set its members apart from others. Sometimes this is done for good reasons, such as when the Bible instructs the High Priest to wear certain garments on specific occasions. Sometimes the reasons are evil, as when the Nazis forced Jews during the Holocaust to wear yellow patches containing the Magen David.

Wearing the button of a political party, the hat of a favorite sports team, the specially colored jacket of your school, a style of shirt or blouse that marks you as "in"—all these are examples of how clothing reflects your identity. Because of the important role clothes play in establishing and conveying one's identity, Judaism has much to say about how you dress and what you wear.

A HISTORICAL PERSPECTIVE

The Shulḥan Arukh says:

It is not permitted to follow the customs of the pagans or to be like them in the way they dress, cut their hair or the like; as it is said, "And you shall not walk in the customs of the nations" (Lev. 20:23). . . .

You shall not say, "Because [people of other nations] walk about dressed in [the royal color of] purple, I, too, will walk about dressed in purple; because they walk about in helmets, I, too, will walk about helmeted." For these are the ways of the proud and the haughty . . . (Sif. Deut. 12:30).

One reason why the ancient Hebrews adopted a strict dress code was to keep their identity very clear. Wearing different clothing helped separate the Jews from the rest of society, preventing them from becoming hopelessly intermingled with the pagans. Today we understand the idea of choosing appropriate clothing in a different way. We ask: Is this way of dressing modest and proper?

Jews, who have lived in India for more than seven centuries, dress in Indian fashion but with traditional Jewish tzni'ut.

Living in the modern world, Ḥasidic Jews dress in a style that dates to the 17th century.

Only a century ago, most people owned few clothes. A Jew might have had one or two outfits for weekdays and a special outfit for Shabbat and holidays. Today, people may own many outfits, so that dressing means making many small decisions about how you are going to look and how you are going to feel during the day.

DRESSING JEWISHLY

You may never have thought about it, but there is actually a Jewish way of dressing. Considering and choosing what you are going to wear from a Jewish point of view is another way we remind ourselves of our Jewish tradition.

For example, Jewish tradition prefers that clothing not cost too much. Why? Because expensive clothing gives you false pride, the feeling that you are somehow better than other people. The danger in false pride is that you will forget that everyone is created in the image of HaShem. Wearing very expensive clothing tempts you to treat people who cannot afford such garments as inferior. That is definitely not a Jewish approach to life.

Yet there are times when it is proper to wear more expensive clothing. On Shabbat, for example, we wear our best clothing. Jews often refer to our best outfits as our "Shabbat clothes," even if we also wear them on other occasions. A wedding, a bar mitzvah, a party—all these events are proper times for dressing splendidly. The clothing we wear at these times honors these special occasions. It is meant to set these moments apart from the other moments of our lives, not to make other people feel unworthy or inadequate.

Jewish law also says you should avoid wearing clothes that look tattered or dirty. The reason is that you are created in the image of HaShem. We know that being created in HaShem's image is more a

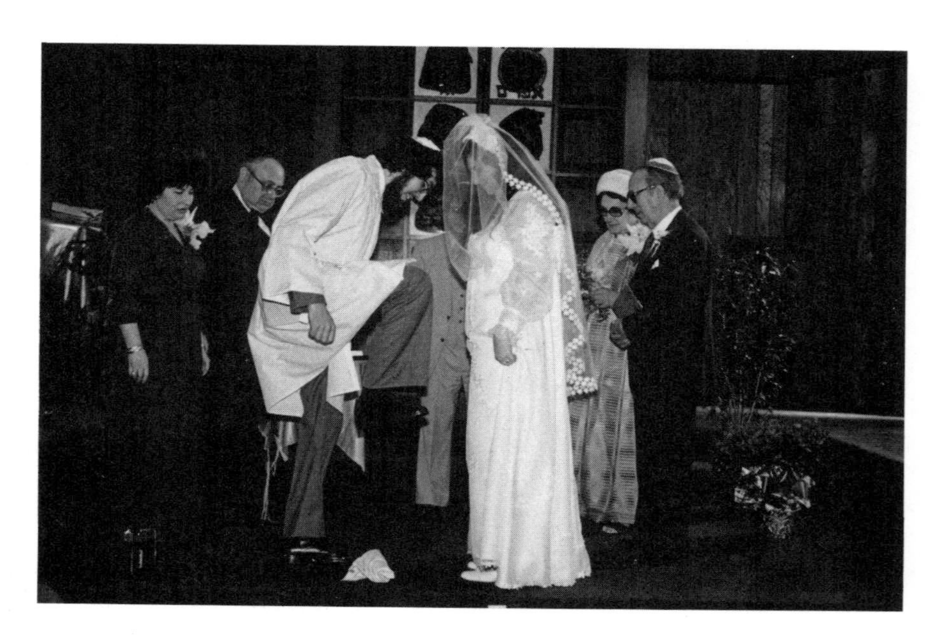

Wearing splendid clothing at festive times is an example of *hiddur mitzvah*, beautifying the commandment.

A team uniform says something important about the identity of the people who wear it.

matter of inner spirit than of outer appearance. Nevertheless, the world often judges your inner spirit by how you look. What you wear is the first impression you give others of who you are.

In urging you to avoid dirty, stained, or shabby clothing, Judaism differs from some other faiths. Some religions stress poverty. They teach that people should give up everything for God. Hindu holy men, for example, give away just about everything that belongs to them and become beggars. They believe that wearing and owning almost nothing helps make them holy.

Judaism believes HaShem created the good things of the world so that we could enjoy and share them. HaShem brought beauty into the world so that it could be shared, too. Sharing and using the things HaShem created is part of living a full Jewish life. So the Talmud teaches, "Three things enhance a person's spirit: a beautiful home, a beautiful mate, and beautiful clothes" (Ber. 57b). Jews count the beauty in the world as a part of HaShem's blessings for us.

FINDING A BALANCE

The need to make a balanced choice when choosing clothes is summed up by the Rambam:

> The dress of a wise man must be free of stains; he should not wear the apparel of princes, to attract attention, nor the raiment of paupers, which incurs disrespect (M.T., Hilkhot De'ot, Laws of Beliefs, 5:9).

The meaning of the Rambam's statement is clear: generally, you should try to dress in moderately priced, clean, and neat clothing. This kind of clothing protects you from false pride, keeps you from making others feel uncomfortable, and prevents you from appearing not to care about what others think of you. You should also wear clothes that are appropriate for the time and place. Just as you would not wear your dressiest outfit on the soccer field, you should not wear your oldest and plainest clothes to the Shabbat dinner table.

As you stand before the clothes hanging in your closet, you have the opportunity to use a Jewish measure in deciding what to wear. You can choose the clothing that best fits not just the outer you but the inner you as well. The Hebrew word **penimah** (פְּנִימָה), which in Psalm 45:14 actually refers to the interior of a palace, is often used to mean that special inner you, where your true glory resides. Jewish tradition holds that the way you act toward others and the way you dress should express your penimah, your best self.

The relationship between the inner and outer you becomes even clearer in this parable told by the Baal Shem Tov, the great eighteenth-century Ḥasidic teacher and leader. A king was informed that people who were humble and lived simply were given long life. The king changed his royal robes for work clothes, left his palace and went to live in a hut, and issued an order saying that no one should pay any special attention to him. As time went on, however, the king found that he was less humble than before. He was actually proud of living so simply. Then a wise teacher said to him, "Dress like a king and live like a king. Let people bow down before you. If you really wish to be humble, learn to be humble in your heart."

The moral of the parable is that the good things we enjoy can make us too proud of ourselves—but not if we learn to be humble in our hearts.

STYLE, FASHION, AND ḤUKKAT HAGOY

In choosing clothing, many people behave foolishly. They become slaves to fashion and style. They eagerly examine store windows and catalogs for the latest fads.

Advertising suggests that anyone who does not dress in a particular way will not be popular. Magazines imply that the whole world judges you by whether you look like a fashion model. But the Shulḥan Arukh takes a longer view. It asks a Jewish question: When you dress, are you trying to make yourself into something you are not?

This Jewish standard is called **ḥukkat hagoy** (חֻקַּת הַגּוֹי), "the law of the nations." Ḥukkat hagoy is actually a negative standard, telling us what we should do by warning us about what we should avoid. It comes from Leviticus 20:23, "And you shall not walk in the customs of the [other] nations." Ḥukkat hagoy tells us that we must not dress in a slavish manner, wearing only and always the same thing that someone else wears. On the other hand, ḥukkat hagoy does not mean that Jews must do exactly the opposite of all other people. That, too, would be a kind of slavery. People who *never* make independent decisions about what to wear are saying something about themselves, just as surely as are those who *always* wear outrageous clothing. The best path to follow is somewhere between these two extremes. And that is exactly the path which Jewish tradition follows.

Simply put, when fashions become outrageous, Jews should have better sense than to follow them. If you slavishly follow fashion, you must ask yourself this serious question: Am I doing this to make others think I am not a Jew? HaShem has commanded us, saying, "I have set you apart from the [other] peoples" (Lev. 20:26). "Apart" means that you should always remember to make your own decisions—decisions that fit with what you truly believe as a Jew.

You may ask: "What's so bad about dressing fashionably? Why shouldn't I wear my hair in the latest style?" If such styles are appropriate for the climate and occasion, they may be perfectly acceptable. But if they are exotic or intended to attract undue attention, you need to ask yourself honestly why you choose to wear them.

Some people follow fashion just to be popular. Judaism tells us that popularity should come from acting in ways that earn the genuine respect of others—not in dressing the way others dress. Some people follow fashion to hide the fact that they are Jewish. Such people don't want others to think of them as different. They seldom fool anyone. People usually see past fashion and identify the Jew inside.

Judaism demands that you be honest with yourself. A person who is only imitating others soon loses respect for himself. A person who follows others just to look like them soon forgets himself. A Jew who seeks always to be like the peoples of the other nations soon forgets to act Jewishly. Judaism says: Be yourself. Act Jewishly.

Ḥasidic Jews often dress in ways which clearly distinguish them from the rest of society. Is their way of dressing more religious than clothes more in keeping with modern fashion? Many Ḥasidic Jews dress in black, never in red, and in the style of eighteenth-century Eastern Europeans. Their dress does not necessarily make them more

Students dressed in Yemenite style perform a Shabbat dance at the Los Angeles Jewish Festival.

A Jewish Best-Dressed List

These ten rules summarize the Jewish approach to dressing the way HaShem, the most original Designer for all time, wants us to dress.

1. *Dress with tzni'ut.* Never dress to expose your body or to stimulate or arouse the opposite sex. Be a **tzanu'a** (צָנוּעַ), an intelligent, discreet person—a high term of praise in the Jewish vocabulary.

2. *Dress with dignity.* Be understated, not ostentatious. "Walk modestly with your God" (Micah 6:8).

3. *Dress discreetly.* Let your actions speak more loudly than your clothes. Gaudy is not Godly.

4. *Dress appropriately.* Be guided by the place and the occasion, not merely by whim. At synagogue or at a simḥah, honor special events with special clothing.

5. *Do not dress to make others feel inferior.* Be proud of what you wear, but not so proud as to want to outshine others, especially the less fortunate.

6. *Do not dress shabbily.* There is no virtue in wearing the cheapest clothing you can find. You are what you wear.

7. *Do not dress sloppily.* Recognize the difference between casual and sloppy. You can dress informally for recreation or relaxation, but even casual clothes should show dignity, discretion, and tzni'ut.

8. *Never wear stained clothes.* Let everything you wear reflect the fact that you were created in the image of HaShem.

9. *Follow religious guidelines.* Observe the traditions for covering the head. Do not wear leather shoes on Yom Kippur. Follow the prohibitions in the Torah (Lev. 19:19, Deut. 22:11) against wearing **sha'atnez** (שַׁעַטְנֵז), fabrics that mix wool and linen.

10. *Remember ḥukkat hagoy.* Do not dress to hide the fact that you are Jewish. You may dress stylishly, but not with the express purpose of looking like everyone else. "And you shall not walk in the customs of the [other] nations" (Lev. 20:23).

religious, but it does proclaim unmistakably their decision to remain separate. That should be their privilege, just as it is the privilege of Roman Catholic priests and nuns to wear their own distinctive garb at religious services and in the street.

DRESSING WITH TZNI'UT

By far the most significant standard for dressing Jewishly is modesty, or **tzni'ut** (צְנִיעוּת). Tzni'ut in this sense means sexual integrity. Clothing designed to expose or highlight parts of the body in order to attract or arouse the opposite sex is prohibited by Jewish law. Supertight jeans on men and short skirts and plunging necklines on women violate the sensitivities that Jews have developed over the centuries.

Some people argue that today is different. Perhaps you say, "I don't wear these clothes to excite or arouse—I just want to look fashionable. Where's the harm in that?"

Judaism answers that blindly following the fashions of the times is not harmless. The laws of tzni'ut are a reflection of a morality that Judaism holds dear. It is not merely possible but preferable to look good while showing tzni'ut in your choice of clothing. Dressing with tzni'ut tells the world that you are a person of sound values and solid upbringing. Flashy clothes that stimulate and excite convey just the opposite impression. That is why observant Jewish women traditionally wear somewhat higher necklines, somewhat longer sleeves, and somewhat longer skirts than other women, and why Jewish men and women avoid skintight jeans and slacks.

CLOTHING AND GENDER

Tzni'ut also means: Be true to your sex. In society and before the law, in the pay they receive and the honors they are accorded, and in the care we give them—in all these things, men and women should be equal. Neither sex is inferior or superior to the other, yet they are undeniably different, and we should not try to blur the differences. The Torah commands, "A woman shall not wear things [normally] worn by a man . . . neither shall a man put on a woman's dress" (Deut. 22:5). This is one reason many Orthodox Jewish women do not wear pants. In our times, pants are the kind of clothing that men usually wear.

Another reason why these women do not wear pants is that when the pants are tightly tailored they tend to be immodest. Orthodox women who choose to wear pants do so in the belief that pants cut distinctively for women may be acceptable. In 1987 the Sephardi chief rabbi of Israel, Ovadiah Yosef, noted that pants are often less exposing than some fashions in women's skirts.

Jewish laws regarding differences between men and women apply to more than just the clothes we wear. Men should not wear women's jewelry or makeup, nor should a man shave his beard if his only reason for shaving is to make his face more like a woman's.

Both men and women are created in HaShem's image. But you may ask, "How can that be when they are so very different?" Actually, all people are created in HaShem's image, although all of us appear different.

People stamp many coins with the same die, and they are all like to one another; but HaShem has stamped every person with the die of the first person, yet not one of them is like any other. Therefore every person must say, "For my sake was the world created" (Sanh. 4:5).

When a man tries to be like a woman, or a woman tries to be like a man, what they are really saying is that HaShem's will is less important than theirs. Trying to act or dress like the opposite sex is a way of denying HaShem. Such behavior reveals that the image you want is more important than the image HaShem has given you. But you were not created by accident. HaShem has a purpose for you and created you to fulfill that purpose. You cannot change your purpose the way you change your clothing.

YIRAT SHAMAYIM

Like all other groups, we Jews have distinctive ways of dressing. We even use special Jewish clothing—kippah, tallit, and tefillin. More than fashion or style, more than the clothes we wear every day, these special forms of clothing enable us to establish our identity as Jews.

Perhaps you have seen men take their hats off when they enter a building. In the Western tradition, taking the hat off is a sign of respect. Our Jewish tradition is just the opposite. It requires men to cover their heads as a way of showing respect for HaShem. In Hebrew, this respect is called **yirat shamayim** (יִרְאַת שָׁמַיִם), the "fear" or "honor" of heaven. One way men show their respect for HaShem is by wearing the **kippah** (כִּפָּה), known in Yiddish as a yarmulke.

In biblical times, Jews did not normally wear a kippah. But the sages of the Talmud regularly covered their heads as a sign of yirat shamayim, and head covering became a Jewish mark of piety and learning.

The kippah is worn as a sign of respect, or yirat shamayim.

This married teacher covers her head as an expression both of yirat shamayim and of tzni'ut. Many married women follow the tradition of exposing their hair only to their husbands.

Rabbi Naḥman said, May I be rewarded for observing the rule of eating three meals on the Sabbath. Rab Judah said, May I be rewarded for observing devotion in prayers. Rabbi Huna ben Rabbi Joshua said, May I be rewarded for never walking four cubits without a head covering (Shab. 118b). . . .

Astrologers told the mother of Rabbi Naḥman ben Isaac, "Your son will be a thief." [Thereupon] she would not let him go bareheaded. She said to him, "Cover your head so that the fear of heaven may be upon you" (Shab. 156b).

In Babylonia the reader of Torah, or **ḥazzan** (חַזָּן), and the kohanim who pronounced the priestly blessing for the congregation covered their heads. Soon the rabbis required all Jews to wear a head covering. In the seventeenth century, the Taz said that since most non-Jews pray bareheaded, Jews should cover their heads in prayer because of ḥukkat hagoy. Long before, in twelfth-century Spain, Rambam wrote that a bareheaded person was often given to silliness, or **kallut rosh** (קַלּוּת רֹאשׁ), which literally means "lightheadedness." Going without a head covering, he said, was to be avoided (M.T., Sefer Hamada, Hilkhot De'ot, 5:6).

In ancient times, women covered their heads with scarves, often masking their faces with veils. Through the ages, Jewish women covered their hair, but Ashkenazic girls went bareheaded until they were married. (Among Sephardic Jews, even young girls covered their hair.) Today, many married Orthodox women cover their hair at all times, and it is common for all married women to cover their heads in the synagogue. Some women wear a wig *(shaytl)* or a kerchief *(tichel)* to cover their heads at all times as a sign of tzni'ut.

A married woman covers her hair to signal to the outside world that she is unavailable for courting. At home, however, in the presence of her husband, there is no such restriction. Married women are encouraged to keep looking attractive to their husbands, in order to strengthen and enrich family life. Married men are likewise responsible for keeping the marriage strong. For example, the rabbis urged that a married man not work in a tannery if that would make him smell so bad that he would be repulsive to his wife when he came home.

TALLIT

In biblical times, most Jews wore a robe with four corners. You can see a similar kind of robe worn by Bedouins today. The Torah commands us to add **tzitzit** (צִיצִית), or fringes, to this robe to remind us of the mitzvot. You repeat this commandment each time you say the Shema:

> The Lord spoke to Moses saying: Speak to the children of Israel and command them to make for themselves tzitzit on the corners of their robes throughout the generations. Let them attach a cord of blue to the tzitzit at each corner. These shall be your tzitzit: look at them and remember all the commandments of the Lord and observe them, so that you do not follow your heart and eyes in the ways of the evil urge. In this way you shall be reminded to observe all My mitzvot and be holy to your God (Num. 15:37-40).

The passage says "command them to make for themselves tzitzit on the corners of their robes throughout the generations." Since you

An eighth-grader (above) and a skilled artisan (right) practice an ancient art—making tzitzit.

no longer wear clothing with four corners, the **tallit** (טַלִּית), or prayer shawl, is meant to enable you to fulfill this mitzvah.

The tallit is usually white and must be at least large enough to cover most of one's back. It is commonly made of wool or cotton. To remind us of the missing blue threads of the tzitzit, some tallitot are today woven with blue stripes. (In the Middle Ages, almost all tallitot contained black stripes.) In addition, the tallit has a collar called an **atarah** at its top. The Hebrew word עֲטָרָה really means "crown": the part of the prayer shawl worn on the neck and shoulders is the "crown" of the tallit.

The tzitzit are made of white threads, set into holes in each corner of the tallit, and knotted in a special way. If you count the Hebrew consonants of the word **ציצית** as numbers, they add up to 600. Add to this the eight threads and the five knots of the tzitzit and the total is 613—the number of mitzvot in the Torah. This is another way in which the tzitzit remind us of the commandments.

Because the idea of tzitzit is to remind us at all times of the mitzvot, Jewish men and boys should wear a squared cloth under the shirt. This cloth, which has fringes at each corner, is sometimes also called tzitzit, but its proper name is **tallit katan** (טַלִּית קָטָן, "small tallit"). Before putting on the tallit katan we say:

בָּרוּךְ אַתָּה, יהוה אֱלֹהֵינוּ, מֶלֶךְ הָעוֹלָם, אֲשֶׁר קִדְּשָׁנוּ בְּמִצְוֹתָיו וְצִוָּנוּ
עַל מִצְוַת צִיצִית.

Blessed are You, Lord, our God, King of the universe, who has sanctified us through His commandments and has commanded us regarding the mitzvah of tzitzit.

The blue thread of the tallit reminds us of the robes which kings and princes wore in ancient times. At first, the blue thread mentioned in the Torah was made with an expensive dye extracted from rare Mediterranean snail shells. When knowledge of the specific organism that produces this dye was lost, and Jews no longer remembered the exact color of the blue, the fringe was made entirely white.

The commandment calls on us to look at the tzitzit. The rabbis said this means we must view them by natural light, the light of day. So men wear the outer tallit during the morning prayers (Shaḥarit), except on Tisha b'Av. On this special day, when we mourn the loss of the Temple, the tallit is not worn until the afternoon. On Yom Kippur, to signify the special holiness of the day, the tallit is worn for every service, beginning with the evening Kol Nidre service.

In some communities only married men wear the outer tallit. Other communities make special tallitot for children. The tallit is such an important mark of our Jewishness that men are usually buried wearing the tallit they used in their lifetimes. Before burial the fringes are removed or torn, since the dead can no longer perform the mitzvah of looking at them.

May women wear the tallit? The Talmud tells us that Rabbi Judah the Prince attached tzitzit to the aprons of the women in his

Tallit and Tefillin: A Poet's View

The Hebrew poet Avraham Shlonsky wrote "Toil" in 1927. In this poem, Shlonsky uses tallit and tefillin as images to describe the holiness of building the homeland and tilling its soil.

My country wraps itself in light as in a tallit.
Houses stand out like tefillin.
And like tefillin straps, the highways that palms have paved glide down.
Here the beautiful town prays Shaḥarit to its creator. . . .

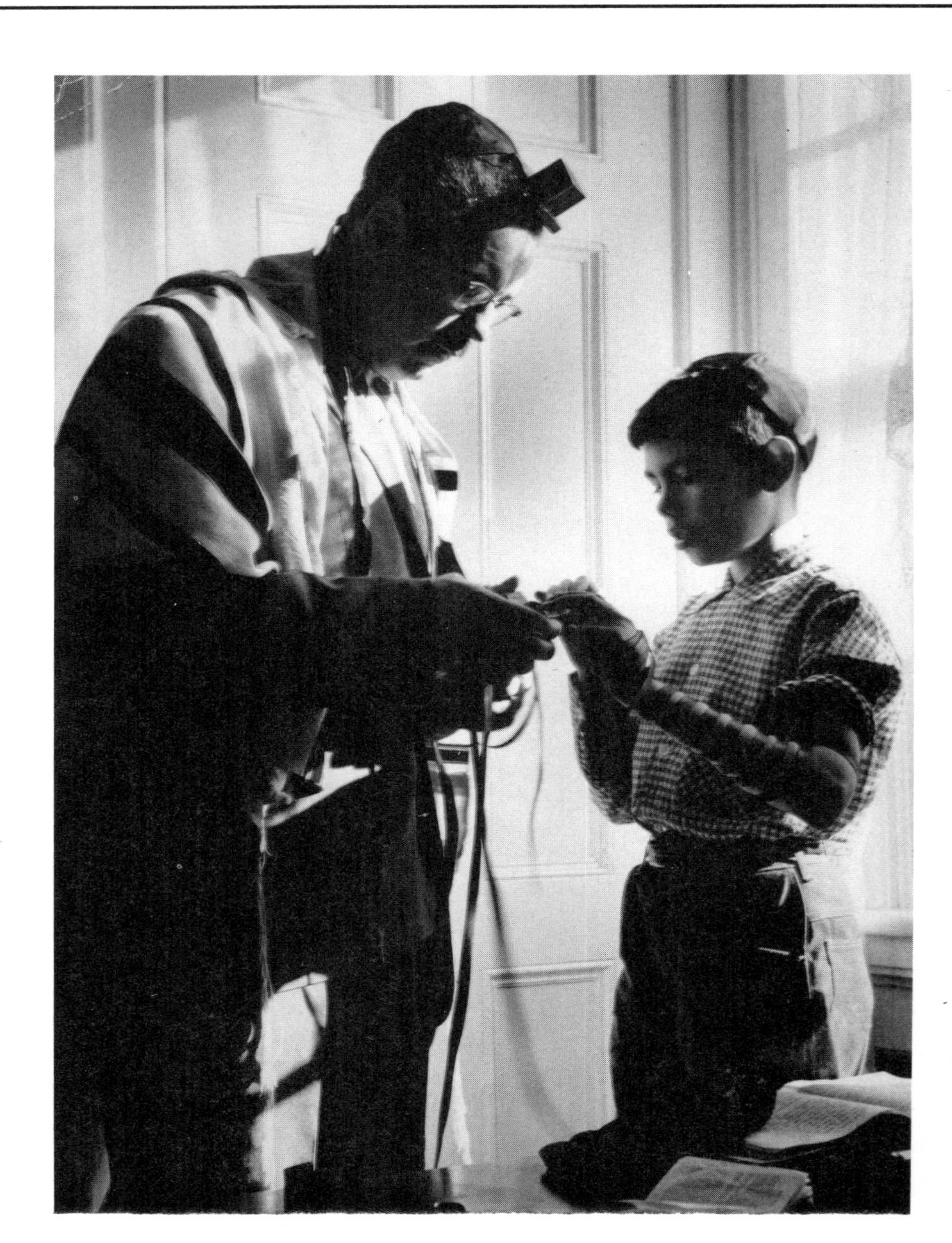

One of the privileges of being bar mitzvah is wearing tefillin every weekday. Although it is preferable to daven as part of a minyan, some men fulfill the mitzvah of tefillin by putting them on at home.

household. He believed the commandment was binding on women as well as men (Men. 43a). Through the ages, however, almost all rabbis have agreed that tallit is one of the commandments that must be done at a set time—only during daytime—in fulfillment of the request that we "look at" the tzitzit. Because women are exempt from commandments that must be performed at a set time, the tradition has held that the mitzvah of tallit need not be observed by women. Thus, in Orthodox synagogues, women do not wear the tallit.

To fulfill the mitzvah of tallit, we begin by reciting a berakhah:

בָּרוּךְ אַתָּה, יהוה אֱלֹהֵינוּ, מֶלֶךְ הָעוֹלָם, אֲשֶׁר קִדְּשָׁנוּ בְּמִצְוֹתָיו וְצִוָּנוּ לְהִתְעַטֵּף בַּצִּיצִית.

Blessed are You, Lord, our God, King of the universe, who has sanctified us through His commandments and has commanded us to wrap ourselves in tzitzit.

First the tallit is put over the head, with all four corners thrown over the left shoulder. Then two corners are put on each side of the body—two in front, on either side, and two in back. On weekdays, we put on the tallit before putting on the tefillin. In some places, men pray with the tallit covering their heads.

The beauty of the mitzvah of tallit has been compared with the mitzvah of dwelling in the sukkah on Sukkot and with the mitzvah of making aliyah to Eretz Yisrael. These are mitzvot you can "step into" and "be embraced by," surrounding you with a special feeling of holiness. Wrapping the tallit around yourself gives you the feeling of being wrapped in HaShem's embrace.

TEFILLIN

While the tallit began as a robe worn every day, the **tefillin** (תְּפִלִּין) had no original practical use. In fact, the only real use of tefillin is in Jewish prayer. So every part of the tefillin is meant to teach you something about being Jewish or praying Jewishly. In fact, the word "tefillin" comes from the same Hebrew root which gives us the word for prayer, **tefillah** (תְּפִלָּה).

Wearing the tefillin shows the world that HaShem is with you: "All the nations of the earth shall see that You are called by the name of the Lord" (Deut. 28:10). The rabbis explained that "the name of the Lord" in this verse refers to the letter ש, which is stamped on the headpiece and which is the first letter of God's name **Shaddai** (שַׁדַּי), the Almighty. For this reason, you do not cover the headpiece, not even with the tallit.

Rambam believed that the tefillin should be worn all day long. Many of the sages of the Mishnah wore them the whole day to show that they bore **ol malkhut shamayim** (עוֹל מַלְכוּת שָׁמַיִם), "the yoke of the Kingdom of Heaven." In time, however, only very pious Jews wore the tefillin all day, and by Rambam's era most Jews wore them only when davening. One of the special privileges of becoming a bar mitzvah is being able to fulfill the command of wearing tefillin every day.

The tefillin are put on just after the tallit. We are commanded to wear the tallit every day, the tefillin on weekdays only. The tefillin consist of leather straps attached to two small leather boxes called **batim** (בָּתִּים), or "houses." One of the batim is worn on the arm, the other on the forehead. Each **bayit** (בַּיִת) contains four passages from the Bible, written by hand on parchment. These are the first two paragraphs of the Shema and two paragraphs taken from the Book of Exodus which refer to the tefillin as a sign of the Exodus and a memorial to it.

The handpiece is worn on the left arm on a level with the heart, to remind you that you must serve God "with all your heart, with all your soul, and with all your might." The leather strap is wound seven times around the forearm, to show that you remember the commandments every day of the week. It is wound three times around the middle finger as a kind of "marriage ring" to HaShem, recalling the three "wedding" promises made by HaShem to the Jewish people in the Book of Hosea (2:21-22):

I will betroth you to Me for ever;
Yea, I will betroth you to Me in righteousness, and in justice, in loving-kindness and in compassion.
And I will betroth you to Me in faithfulness;
So you shall know the Lord.

The handpiece is put on first, followed by the headpiece. After putting the first bayit on the arm, but before tightening the strap around the biceps, you recite the berakhah,

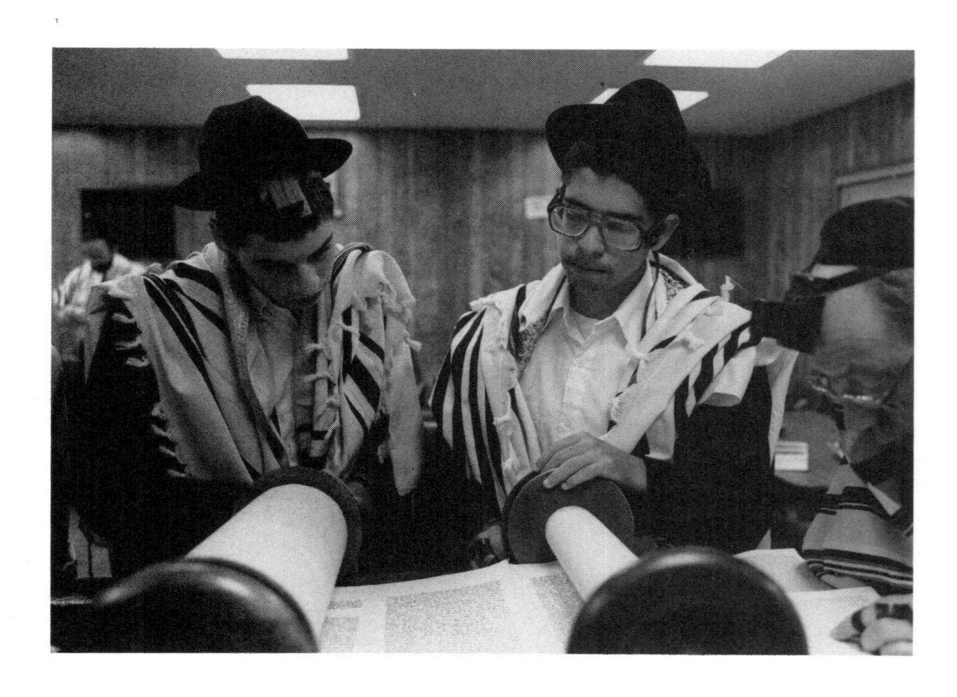

Tefillin are worn during Shaḥarit, which on Mondays and Thursdays includes a short Torah reading.

בָּרוּךְ אַתָּה, יהוה אֱלֹהֵינוּ, מֶלֶךְ הָעוֹלָם, אֲשֶׁר קִדְּשָׁנוּ בְּמִצְוֹתָיו וְצִוָּנוּ לְהַנִּיחַ תְּפִלִּין.

Blessed are You, Lord, our God, King of the universe, who has sanctified us through His commandments and has commanded us to wear tefillin.

Next, the bayit of the headpiece is placed on the forehead above the space between the eyes, as the commandment states. Its two straps are allowed to fall to either side. Before putting it into place, you say the berakhah,

בָּרוּךְ אַתָּה, יהוה אֱלֹהֵינוּ, מֶלֶךְ הָעוֹלָם, אֲשֶׁר קִדְּשָׁנוּ בְּמִצְוֹתָיו וְצִוָּנוּ עַל מִצְוַת תְּפִלִּין.

Blessed are You, Lord, our God, King of the universe, who has sanctified us through His commandments and has commanded us regarding the mitzvah of tefillin.

Then you recite these words:

בָּרוּךְ שֵׁם כְּבוֹד מַלְכוּתוֹ לְעוֹלָם וָעֶד.

Blessed be His glorious Kingdom for ever and ever.

The tefillin touch your head, arm, and hand, and are close to your eyes and your heart. Together with the kippah and tallit, they are a reminder that you must serve HaShem in all you think and do.

CHAPTER THREE

DAVENING

דע לפני מי אתה עומד.

Know before Whom you stand.

(Ber. 28b)

Jews have always prayed. In the Torah, Abraham pleads with HaShem on behalf of Sodom and Gomorrah; Isaac asks HaShem for the blessing of a child; Jacob asks HaShem to protect him from the hands of Esau; and the Jewish people pray to be set free from Egyptian slavery. Moses asks HaShem to cure Miriam, his sister. Hannah prays to HaShem for a child, and Samuel the prophet is born.

Prayer, or **tefillah** (תְּפִלָּה), is a universal expression. People pray when they are frightened, when they feel alone, when they need help, or when they want to give thanks for something special. Tefillah connects you both to heaven and to the world. Making tefillah a regular part of your life is both a personal need and a Jewish requirement. No one can live a full Jewish life without tefillah.

The Hebrew word **hitpallel** (הִתְפַּלֵּל), usually translated as "to pray," actually means "to judge oneself." This implies stepping back from active life in order to gain a true assessment of yourself and your relationship to HaShem and the world. The process leading to such self-judgment is called tefillah.

In English we usually translate tefillah as "prayer," but this word does not fully express the concept. "Praying" is commonly understood to mean asking for something, yet that is only a small piece of the grand idea of tefillah. The word for prayer most commonly used by Jews is **daven**, a Yiddish term based on the French word *devant*. In French, *devant* means "before," as in standing "before" HaShem. In Yiddish the word became *daven*, and to English-speaking Jews the process of praying became known as **davening**. All davening involves standing before HaShem in order to communicate with Him.

TEFILLAH IN JEWISH LIFE

The rabbis, who understood the importance of tefillah, composed not only the Amidah but also the Kiddush, Havdalah, and many other tefillot. Other rabbis added more prayers as time went on, and the tradition of composing and adding prayers that responded to the community's needs or to personal crises finally led to the **siddur** (סִדּוּר), or Jewish prayer book, as we have it today.

The language of tefillah binds all Jews as one people the world over. Above, Israeli soldiers davening in Lebanon in 1982; in the midst of war they recite Sim Shalom, a prayer for peace. At right, standing before the Aron HaKodesh and before HaShem in Mississippi.

On a weekday in Jerusalem, a bar mitzvah ceremony in the company of strangers and friends——all one family.

Jews have prayers, or **tefillot** (תְּפִלּוֹת), for almost every occasion, and we are allowed to daven almost anywhere we feel like davening. Nevertheless, the basic Jewish prayers may not be spoken whenever we wish. They must be said at certain times and in the appropriate manner.

Why is this so? Why can't you just say the tefillot only when you feel especially close to HaShem—for example, when you are looking at the ocean or at a beautiful sunset? The answer is that you cannot leave something as important as tefillah to chance or impulse. It is natural to feel close to HaShem when you look at an ocean or a sunset. But how long has it been since you did that? When you daven regularly, at the correct time and with the proper tefillot, you train your soul, and the feeling of genuine closeness to HaShem comes often.

The biblical source for the obligation to pray is the verse "And you shall serve the Lord your God" (Ex. 23:25). We know that "serve" means "pray" because the Torah adds "with all your heart." The duty to daven is central to Jewish life, equally binding, in different ways, on both men and women.

How and why are women's prayer obligations different from men's? Women have the same right and the same obligation to daven as do men. But since women also have to nurse infants (a unique biological gift from HaShem), feed the family, and care for the most important things in family life, the Torah could not impose upon them another set of time regulations, as it could upon men. Even if individual women could spare the time every single morning, the halakhah considered the natural needs and abilities of the general public, and did not decide any law on the basis of a select few.

The Torah makes it clear that all human beings must look to HaShem for blessings, asking Him for help in the world He created. Since it would be impossible to go through any single day without finding some need for a blessing from HaShem, it follows automatically that all of us—women and men—must daven every day. In this sense, then, tefillah is a Torah commandment, while the particular times and places for davening are decisions of the sages. A woman's obligation of daily tefillah may be fulfilled by her own prayers once a day, according to some sages, and with formal prayer morning and night, according to others.

Maimonides—the Rambam—believed that tefillah is *d'oraita*, commanded by the Torah, for every Jew, man or woman, once a day.

Both women and men have the right and the duty to daven.

The Amidah

The **Amidah** (עֲמִידָה), with variations, is the heart of all Jewish religious services, including Shaḥarit, Minḥah, and Ma'ariv. So central is the Amidah to Jewish worship that when the Talmud speaks of tefillah, the Amidah is what it means. The Amidah has long been known as the "Eighteen Blessings"—in Hebrew, **Shemoneh Esreh** (שְׁמוֹנֶה עֶשְׂרֵה) literally means "eighteen"—although nineteen separate blessings are now included.

On Shabbat and holidays we use only the first three and the last three blessings of the Amidah. On these days the thirteen intermediate blessings—which are really requests for blessings from HaShem—are replaced by a particular blessing designed to sanctify the specialness of the occasion.

FIRST THREE BLESSINGS (WEEKDAYS AND SHABBAT)

1. Avot (אָבוֹת): "Fathers"; includes verses from Exodus, Deuteronomy, Nehemiah, Genesis, and Leviticus. In this blessing we identify ourselves as children of the Patriarchs.

2. Gevurot (גְבוּרוֹת): "Powers"; includes verses from Psalms, Daniel, and Samuel. In this blessing we recognize HaShem's power to sustain and change the world.

3. Kedushat HaShem (קְדוּשַּׁת הַשֵּׁם): "HaShem's Holiness"; when a minyan is present, the Kedushah is recited during the public repetition of the Amidah.

THIRTEEN INTERMEDIATE REQUEST BLESSINGS (WEEKDAYS ONLY)

4. Binah (בִּינָה): "Understanding"; requests knowledge, wisdom, and insight, the basis for the religious life.

5. Teshuvah (תְּשׁוּבָה): "Repentance"; asks HaShem to allow us to return to His Torah and His service, which follows from true understanding.

6. Seliḥah (סְלִיחָה): "Forgiveness"; requests absolution for sins we may have committed in the recent past.

7. Ge'ula (גְאוּלָּה): "Redemption"; seeks an end to personal agony and national crisis. Following this blessing on fast days we insert the prayer **Aneinu** (עֲנֵנוּ), "Answer Us."

8. Refu'ah (רְפוּאָה): "Healing"; asks the Divine Healer to relieve all manner of sickness. In this blessing we insert the names of those who are ill and plead for their recovery.

9. Birkat HaShanim (בִּרְכַּת הַשָּׁנִים): "Prosperity"; asks HaShem to grant us material success. From early December to the first day of Pesaḥ, the request specifically calls for the "dew and rain" the earth requires in order to produce an abundant harvest.

10. Kibbutz Galuyot (קִבּוּץ גָּלֻיּוֹת): "Ingathering of the Exiles"; asks for the return of the Jewish people to Eretz Yisrael.

11. Birkat HaMishpat (בִּרְכַּת הַמִּשְׁפָּט): "Restoration of Justice"; requests HaShem to restore righteous judges and to reign over Israel.

12. Birkat HaMinim (בִּרְכַּת הַמִּינִים): "Destruction of Enemies"; a malediction calling upon HaShem to punish the wicked, humble the arrogant, and crush the enemies of Israel.

13. Birkat HaTzaddikim (בִּרְכַּת הַצַּדִּיקִים): "Blessing for the Righteous"; asks HaShem to have compassion for the pious, the saintly, the scholars, the leaders of the House of Israel, and all those who have sincerely embraced Judaism.

14. Birkat Yerushalayim (בִּרְכַּת יְרוּשָׁלַיִם): "Rebuilding of Jerusalem"; requests HaShem to dwell in Jerusalem. During Minḥah on Tisha b'Av we add a request that HaShem comfort those who mourn the destruction of Zion and the ancient Temple.

15. Birkat David (בִּרְכַּת דָּוִד): "For the Restoration of the Kingdom of David"; a prayer for a return to Davidic rule and, through it, for the coming of Mashiaḥ.

16. Shome'a Tefillah (שׁוֹמֵעַ תְּפִלָּה): "Hear Our Prayer"; the last of the thirteen petitions, expressing the hope that HaShem hears us and compassionately accepts our prayers. In this blessing we insert personal prayers for our livelihood and for forgiveness of sins, as well as a special prayer in time of drought.

FINAL THREE BLESSINGS (WEEKDAYS AND SHABBAT)

17. Avodah (עֲבוֹדָה): "Worship"; calls for the restoration of the ancient Temple of Jerusalem. Here we insert the **Ya'aleh V'Yavo** (יַעֲלֶה וְיָבֹא) prayer at the new moon and on the intermediate days of festivals.

18. Birkat Hoda'ah (בִּרְכַּת הוֹדָאָה): "Thanksgiving"; an expression of profound gratitude to HaShem for His daily miracles. On Ḥanukkah and Purim we make special mention of the miracles HaShem performed for us at those times.

19. Birkat Shalom (בִּרְכַּת שָׁלוֹם): "Peace"; asks for HaShem's blessings of tranquillity, goodness, kindness, and mercy for "all of us together." In its full version this concluding prayer includes the kohen's blessing, **Birkat Kohanim** (בִּרְכַּת כֹּהֲנִים).

After the nineteen blessings we append the prayer of the Talmud:

אֱלֹהַי, נְצֹר לְשׁוֹנִי מֵרָע, וּשְׂפָתַי מִדַּבֵּר מִרְמָה.

My God, keep my tongue from speaking evil and my lips from uttering deceit.

He taught that only the time and the form of tefillah are rabbinic —that is, ordained by the sages. Naḥmanides, known as the **Ramban** (for **R**abbi **M**oshe **b**en **N**aḥman), held that all tefillah is rabbinic in authority; he maintained that tefillah is *d'oraita* only in *et tzarah*, in time of trouble or panic.

In our own era, Rabbi Joseph Soloveitchik introduced the important idea that there really was no fundamental disagreement between Rambam and Ramban on this issue. Both Rambam and Ramban believed that prayer in *et tzarah* was sanctioned by the Torah. But because Rambam also believed that we are always in *et tzarah*—that is, always on the edge of crisis—he taught that daily tefillah is *d'oraita*.

SACRIFICES AND TEFILLAH

The earliest universal communications with HaShem were through animal sacrifices. **Korban** (קָרְבָּן), which means "sacrifice," comes from the Hebrew root קרב, meaning "to draw near" or "to come closer." Tefillah through the medium of animal sacrifices was meant to bring us closer to HaShem. In early Jewish history, verbal prayer accompanied the offering but was considered less important than the sacrifice itself.

The laws of sacrifice are spelled out in the Torah and fully discussed in the writings of the rabbis, while the laws of tefillah are only found from the time of the rabbis of the Talmud onward. What caused this change in Jewish life? How did sacrifices give way to verbal prayer as our primary means of addressing HaShem?

The great shift took place when the **Bet HaMikdash** (בֵּית הַמִּקְדָּשׁ), the Temple in Jerusalem, was demolished, and the laws of sacrifice could no longer be fulfilled. Judaism was in grave danger: its very center was in ruins, its capital city in flames, its people driven from the land, its method of communication with HaShem seemingly destroyed.

How could the Jews survive this terrible blow? The first thing they did was to establish a new, even stronger, way of life, without the Bet HaMikdash at its center. This is how they expressed their relationship with HaShem in the absence of the sacrifices:

> **Simeon the Just said, "On three things the world is based: on the Torah, on the Temple service, and on the doing of loving deeds." . . . In regard to the third, it is said, "I desire loving-kindness (ḥesed), not sacrifice." In the beginning the world was created only by ḥesed, as it is said, "The world is built by ḥesed" (Mekhilta, Beshalah, ch. 9).**

According to the Torah, sacrifices could only be offered in the Bet HaMikdash on the Temple Mount. It was forbidden to offer sacrifices anywhere else. How then could people communicate their needs to HaShem? The rabbis addressed this dilemma by declaring that tefillah and deeds of loving-kindness could substitute for the Temple service and its sacrifices. "The sacrifices of God are a broken spirit," they said.

The world cannot encompass the glory of HaShem, but He can be found in a little store-front synagogue on New York's Lower East Side.

Once Rabbi Yoḥanan ben Zakkai and Rabbi Joshua went out from Jerusalem. When Rabbi Joshua saw the burnt ruins of the Temple, he said, "How terrible that the place where the sins of Israel find atonement is laid waste." Rabbi Yoḥanan replied, "Grieve not. We have an atonement equal to the Temple, [and that is] the doing of deeds of loving-kindness (ḥesed), and not sacrifice," as it is said, "I desire ḥesed, not sacrifice" (ARN 4,11).

THREE TIMES A DAY

The three times of daily prayer substitute for the three sacrifices originally offered in the Temple. **Shaḥarit** (שַׁחֲרִית) represents the **korban tamid** (קָרְבָּן תָּמִיד), the daily sacrifice of the morning; **Minḥah** (מִנְחָה) represents the korban tamid of the afternoon; and **Ma'ariv** (מַעֲרִיב) represents the nightly burning of the remains of animals that were left over. The **musaf** (מוּסָף) prayers which we offer on Shabbat and holidays represent the **korban musaf** (קָרְבָּן מוּסָף), the additional sacrifice made in Temple times.

Later, tradition assigned each of the three daily prayer services to one of the patriarchs.

Rabbi Ḥanina said: The daily prayers were instituted by the patriarchs. . . . Abraham established the morning prayer, as it is said, "And Abraham got up early in the morning to the place where he had stood before the Lord" (Gen.

19:27). Isaac [established] the afternoon prayer, as it is said, "And Isaac went out to meditate in the field toward evening" (Gen. 24:63), and meditation means prayer; and Jacob established the evening prayer, as it is said, ". . . and he alighted *(va-yifga)* upon the place and slept there" (Gen. 28:11). And *va-yifga* means prayer (Ber. 26b).

Another explanation for davening three times a day was advanced by the twelfth-century Jewish poet and philosopher Judah HaLevi:

The hour of prayer is the climax, the flowering and the goal, of the day of the pious; all other hours are merely preliminary to it. Thus the three periods of daily prayers are the climax of the day; just as Shabbat is the goal of the week. Prayer is for the soul what food is for the body. The blessing of prayer lasts until the next, just as the strength gained from one meal lasts till the one after. The longer the interval between one prayer and the next, the more a person's soul occupies itself with worldly things—the more it is dulled by them, especially when one is forced to listen to words that dim the purity of the soul. During the time of prayer, however, a person's soul is purged from all that has contaminated it. A person prepares the soul for the future (Kuzari, III, V).

Although the tradition says you should daven three times a day, sometimes events such as a play or soccer game may cause you to miss tefillah. What's so bad about skipping prayers once in a while if it conflicts with some other worthwhile activity?

The answer is that if you let tefillah become haphazard, you may soon forget about it completely; every excuse makes the next lapse easier to excuse. You should make davening as compelling as getting dressed. Get up earlier, plan ahead, work at it, and you will make it happen. If you can't get to services, pray at home. If you can't do the entire service all the time, do almost all of it. Don't settle for "as long as I tried." Eventually, you may stop trying.

THE UNIQUENESS OF TEFILLAH

Rooted both in Jewish history and in Jewish theology, tefillah is basic to Jewish life and spirit. The siddur is not merely a collection of beautiful words by brilliant poets. Each service has its own life—its own place and significance, and its own specific relationship to the time it is recited. Each service has a tone and rhythm all its own.

For example, the early morning service (which follows soon after you "arise like a lion") is expansive and exciting. With the world refreshed and your energy restored, you thank God by saying the **Modeh Ani** (מוֹדֶה אֲנִי), and you raise your voice to daven before HaShem. The Shema is preceded by many psalms, called **pesukei d'zimrah** (פְּסוּקֵי דְזִמְרָה), praising HaShem for the world He created, for nature, for Jewish history. They lift your spirits and prepare you to face your teachers or bosses or friends.

By Minḥah, in late afternoon, the mood has shifted. There is only one psalm, the Amidah, and the concluding prayer. Minḥah is brief, concise, abrupt. The day has taken its toll, sapping your energies. What lies ahead is the night.

Afterward, in the Ma'ariv service, you ask for HaShem's protection. You speak of your trust and faith in HaShem, knowing that He will care for you. A short time later you draw the shades, lock the door, and shut out people and demands. You recite your bedtime prayers and drop off to sleep, unconscious to the world outside.

In the passage of Ma'ariv that follows the Shema, we say in even, measured words:

True and trustworthy is all this. . . . It is He who redeemed us from the power of tyrants. . . . Grant, O Lord our God, that we lie down in peace and that we rise up again. . . .

Contrast the steady pace of that prayer with the passage that follows the morning Shema. Here we explode in a staccato rendition of sixteen adjectives with fifteen "ands" breathlessly inserted between them, until we reach a climactic declaration of faith:

True and certain and established and enduring and right and steadfast and beloved and precious and pleasant and sweet and revered and glorious and correct and acceptable and good and beautiful is this faith to us for ever and ever.

Ahavat Yisrael—love of Israel—thrives in a California beachfront community.

Modes of Prayer

The rabbis found the beginnings of Jewish prayer in the Torah, from which many of the tefillot in the siddur are taken. In the prayer which King Solomon spoke at the dedication of the First Temple, the rabbis identified several kinds of Jewish prayer:

"Praised be the Lord, God of Israel, who has fulfilled with deeds the promise He made to my father David. . . ." Then Solomon stood before the altar of the Lord in the presence of the whole community of Israel; he spread the palms of his hands toward heaven and said, "O Lord God of Israel, in the heavens above and on the earth below there is no God like You, who keeps Your gracious covenant with Your servants when they walk before You in wholehearted devotion; You who have kept the promises You made to Your servant, my father David, fulfilling with deeds the promises You made. . . . Now, therefore, O God of Israel, let the promise that You made to Your servant my father David be fulfilled. . . . Yet turn, O Lord my God, to the prayer and supplication of Your servant, and hear the cry and prayer which Your servant offers before You this day. May Your eyes be open day and night toward this House. . . . And when You hear the pleas which Your servant and Your people Israel offer toward this place, give heed in Your heavenly abode—give heed and pardon" (I Kings 8:15, 22-30).

The rabbis said that in this one prayer Solomon offered praise to HaShem, asked HaShem for help, spoke words of thanksgiving, and confessed his sins and the sins of Israel. The siddur provides examples of each of these four main types of tefillot.

WHY DAVEN IN HEBREW?

Throughout history there have been Jews who did not understand the Hebrew of the tefillot. Even in the time of the rabbis, the spoken language of the Jewish people was Aramaic, and not everyone was able to understand Hebrew. Yet Jews can experience the power of Hebrew prayer even when they do not fully grasp the meaning of the words. Jewish tradition holds that there is a higher value than understanding, and that even when we do not know what the words mean, reciting the words in the right spirit enables us to communicate with HaShem.

The modern Jewish writer and translator Maurice Samuel recalled that one afternoon, while standing near a storefront synagogue on New York's Lower East Side, he heard the sounds of the Minḥah prayers. The shopkeepers, who had hurriedly left their businesses for the fifteen-minute service, seemed to run the words of the prayers together, as in "HappyaretheywhodwellinThyhouse."

"This is absurd," Samuel thought. "They don't even understand what they are saying."

1. PRAISE: "Blessed are You, O Lord our God, King of the universe, who forms light and creates darkness, who makes peace and creates all things. In Your mercy You give light to the earth and its inhabitants. In Your goodness You renew the work of creation every day continually. How manifold are Your works, O Lord! In wisdom have You made them all."

2. INTERCESSION: "You favor man with knowledge and teach human beings understanding. O favor us with Your knowledge, understanding, and discernment. Blessed are You, O Lord, Giver of knowledge."

3. THANKSGIVING: "Though our mouths were full of song as the sea, and our tongues with exultation as the multitude of its waves . . . we should still be unable to thank You and to praise Your name, O Lord our God and God of our fathers, for one thousandth or one ten-thousandth part of the bounties which You have bestowed upon our fathers and upon us."

4. CONFESSION: "For the sin which we have committed before You under compulsion, or of our own will, and for the sin which we have committed before You in hardening of the heart; for the sin which we have committed before You out of ignorance, and for the sin which we have committed before You through words spoken by our lips . . . for all these, O God of forgiveness, forgive us, pardon us, grant us remission."

Years later he realized how blind he had been. Here he was, a modern thinker and writer, who never went to synagogue, because he was always waiting until the spirit moved him and until he understood exactly what each word meant. On the other hand, these shopkeepers, who paid little attention to the individual words, davened three times every day. Each day they lifted their souls to HaShem, and spoke to Him.

Indeed, you should try to discover the meanings of the tefillot. But if you wait for perfect understanding, life will pass you by, and you will never have experienced the magnificence of being intimate with HaShem.

One reason we pray in Hebrew, imperfect as our understanding of it may be, is that the Hebrew of the siddur ties us together with Jews all around the world. Whether you enter a synagogue in Vienna, Buenos Aires, Mexico City, Odessa, or Jerusalem, the prayers are the same. In all these places and hundreds of others, Hebrew is our common tongue, the Jewish language. By drawing us into a common circle with Jews whose native language is different from ours, the language of tefillah binds all Jews as one people the world over.

Under czars and commissars, through decades of difficult times for our people, the minyan has continued at this St. Petersburg synagogue.

This may explain why most Jews use the same tefillot (even if the traditional formulations differ slightly) and recite the same words of Hebrew as other Jews throughout the world. But this explanation does not do justice to the power and beauty of Hebrew prayer. There is natural poetry in the words of the tefillot, to which composed melodies add the poetry of song, and ritual motions add the poetry of dance. All these things lift up our spirits and transport us from our everyday world to a higher reality.

PREPARING TO DAVEN

As a Jew, you do not just start praying. First you must prepare yourself to pray. Tefillah is a serious concern, for in davening you "draw near" to HaShem.

The rabbis said we should rush to the synagogue or the **bet midrash** (בֵּית מִדְרָשׁ, "house of study") because it is always proper to hurry to do a mitzvah. Yet as we reach the door, we should slow down and think before going in. We should realize that we are about to enter into the presence of the King of Kings. We should try to fill ourselves with the feelings that are proper to such an occasion.

Even when you daven privately, at home, you should take care to be properly dressed. This is the kind of honor you would give an earthly king; it is that much more important before the King of Kings. Nor is dressing properly the only way you need to prepare.

It is well to give charity before praying, as it is written, "As for me, in righteousness shall I behold Your face" (Ps. 17:15); and also to resolve to observe the Divine Command, "And you shall love your neighbor as yourself" (Lev. 19:18). For if there is . . . turmoil among the people of Israel on earth, there is no harmony above [in heaven]. Harmony among the people on earth causes unity and agreement of their souls in heaven above. By means of this, their prayers also become united as one, and united into one, they are acceptable before HaShem, Blessed be He (Kitzur S.A. 12,2).

It is also considered customary to wash your hands before praying, even if they are clean. If water is unavailable, you can clean your hands with sand, leaves, wood, or anything else that might be used for scrubbing.

Communal mourning on Tisha b'Av: "Alas! Lonely sits the city. . . . Bitterly she weeps in the night, her cheek wet with tears" (Lam. 1:1-2).

MINYAN

To daven properly you should do so in the company of others, defined by Jewish tradition as a **minyan** (מִנְיָן), a quorum of ten males who are bar mitzvah. The idea that ten make up a minyan is taken from the Book of Numbers, where the word **eidah** (עֵדָה, "congregation") is used to speak of the ten men who brought back evil reports of the Holy Land.

Going to a minyan requires you to set fixed times for tefillah, keeping you constant in your daily duty. Moreover, coming together with others helps to ensure that your tefillah will be acceptable. The rabbis held that even the prayer of a sinful person in the congregation is heard in heaven, for it is joined to the prayer of the whole congregation.

When you daven together with other Jews, HaShem accepts your tefillah among all their tefillot. This idea is also drawn from the Torah. When Abraham bargained with HaShem to save Sodom and Gomorrah, he stopped when HaShem agreed to save the cities if ten good people could be found. So we learn that a community may be saved for the sake of ten good people, but if there are fewer than ten, each person must be judged alone.

When it comes to making a minyan, all men of Israel are equal. According to an old Jewish saying, "Nine rabbis do not make up a minyan, but ten shoemakers do!"

If the time for worship comes and there are not ten men to make up a minyan, the tefillah may still be said, but some prayers—those which sanctify God's Name in public—may not be said. Such tefillot include the Kaddish; the Kedushah; the **Borkhu** (בָּרְכוּ), the invitation to daven; the Birkat Kohanim; the public recital of the Amidah; and the reading of the Torah. At Leviticus 22:32, HaShem says "that I may be sanctified in the midst of the Israelite people." So prayers sanctifying God's Name are recited aloud only in a minyan.

While it is always possible to daven alone in private (**tefillat yahid**, תְּפִלַּת יָחִיד), we miss out on the many advantages of public worship (**tefillah b'tzibbur**, תְּפִלָּה בְּצִבּוּר) if we do not attend a minyan. In the Talmud it is written:

> **Whoever comes to pray in the synagogue or in the bet midrash, morning and evening at the proper time, and stays the appropriate length of time, and behaves with the proper respect, will merit long life, for it is written, "Happy is the one who listens to Me, watching daily at My gates, waiting at the posts of my doors" (Prov. 8:34).**

When you regularly attend the congregational minyan, you take part in a wonderful experience. You look forward to seeing the people you know, members of the congregation who have grown nearly as close to you as your own family. In fact, they are your family—your Jewish family. They look forward to seeing you. They depend on you. Together you face the bad times—when one of the members of the minyan falls ill or loses a loved one. And together you rejoice in the good times—when there is a marriage or bar mitzvah in the family or when one of the members has a new son or daughter. Davening in a minyan is an opportunity to stop acting only as an individual and to become part of something much greater than yourself.

DAVENING WITH KAVANAH

When davening, the most important thing is to say the tefillah with **kavanah** (כַּוָּנָה), a word that can mean direction, intensity, devotion, or concentration. As Rambam noted, "Prayer without devotion is not prayer." If your thoughts are not on what you are saying, if your mind is wandering, your tefillah can hardly rise upward. You must put your whole self into your tefillah. Only then can tefillah become a powerful force in you and in the world.

A wonderful Ḥasidic story shows what happens when people pray without kavanah. The Baal Shem Tov and his students traveled from town to town, stopping to daven in local synagogues. One morning, as they came to the entrance of a particular synagogue, the Baal Shem Tov hesitated, unable to enter. His students asked him why he did not go inside. The Baal Shem Tov replied, "I cannot fit into this place." "But it's almost empty," his Ḥasidim argued. "No, it is much too crowded," he responded. "This synagogue is full of prayers that could never rise to heaven because they were not offered with a whole heart. That is why I cannot squeeze in! A prayer must have wings."

Because tefillah is such an intimate and personal act, it is often called **avodah shebalev** (עֲבוֹדָה שֶׁבַּלֵּב), "the service of the heart." In order for you to feel that your prayers are rising up to heaven, you must offer them with all your heart, with all your soul, with all your might. Otherwise, they are nothing more than words. Remember:

When you daven, just watching or listening or reading isn't enough. Davening is something you become part of. The words may have been written somewhere else, by someone else, but at the moment you speak them, you must feel they are *your* words.

Describing tefillah as avodah shebalev raises an interesting question. If tefillah is so personal, why can't we just make up our own words of prayer? The rabbis knew that even the brightest and most gifted person cannot always find the perfect words to say while davening. If the real purpose of tefillah is to give you a way of talking with HaShem, then it is probably better for you to use words composed by King David than to search constantly for words of your own. For this reason, through the centuries, Jews have taken the finest prayers and collected them in the siddur. To make your tefillah even more personal, there are set places in the Shemoneh Esreh when you can add your own words of prayer. Women usually offer their personal prayer at candle lighting, at the onset of Shabbat. They should offer a personal prayer every day, according to Rambam.

IN THE BET KNESSET

As you look deep inside yourself for kavanah while davening, the synagogue itself can help you. It is a place of sanctity, a place devoted to tefillah.

Look around you. Before you is the **Aron HaKodesh** (אֲרוֹן הַקֹּדֶשׁ), the Holy Ark, containing the scrolls of the Torah. Above it burns the

Tefillat Shav

The Jewish tradition strenuously avoids certain types of prayers. These "useless prayers" address something that has already been determined. The name for such a prayer is **tefillat shav** (תְּפִלַּת שָׁוְא).

The Mishnah says:

To pray for what is past is a vain prayer. How is this? His wife was pregnant and he said, "May it be Your will that my wife will bear a male child"—this is a useless prayer. He was coming [home] from a journey and heard a cry of anguish in the city and said, "May it be Your will that the people crying are not my family"—this is a useless prayer (Ber. 9:3).

In the nineteenth century, Rabbi Akiva Eger wrote:

One should not pray to God for something which contradicts the laws of nature. . . . And it is also forbidden to pray that God should perform a miracle which will alter the rules of nature—that a tree will bear fruit before its time.

ner tamid (נֵר תָּמִיד), the Eternal Light, which reminds us that HaShem watches over us all the time. The **bimah** (בִּימָה), the altar of the synagogue, recalls the altar of sacrifice in the Holy Temple.

Moreover, the synagogue is not just a building. We call it the **bet knesset** (בֵּית כְּנֶסֶת), the house of assembly. It is a second home for its members, the congregation. Just a quick look at the prayers in the siddur shows that almost all of them are "we"-centered: they are virtually all in the plural. Together we praise HaShem for His love and compassion. Together we confess our weaknesses and ask HaShem for forgiveness. Together we say the **Hallel** (הַלֵּל) on special days, singing psalms of praise and thanksgiving. Together we ask HaShem to give us the things we need to make our community better—wisdom, health, and peace. Together, three days a week, we study the Torah in the midst of our prayers.

An intense moment of personal prayer—avodah shebalev—at the women's section of the Western Wall. Jews of all kinds gather here to daven where the Bet HaMikdash once stood.

BERAKHAH

Jewish prayer has grown from the series of blessings that form the Amidah into a complete and beautiful liturgy filled with melody and movement. Through davening you can discover the deeper meaning of the simple formula called **berakhah** (בְּרָכָה), or "blessing."

בָּרוּךְ אַתָּה, יהוה אֱלֹהֵינוּ, מֶלֶךְ הָעוֹלָם
Blessed are You, Lord, our God, King of the universe, who . . .

These are the basic words of the berakhah. Through these words we celebrate the world HaShem created and the laws He has instructed us to observe. The berakhah begins by addressing HaShem in personal terms: "Blessed are You, Lord. . . ." A moment later, we speak of HaShem in the third person: "Our God, King of the world, who. . . ." What accounts for this shift in tone and grammar? Is HaShem personal—a friend, a partner, a companion? Or is HaShem distant—a king, a creator, a commander? The berakhah seems to want it both ways, and in truth, both ways are right. HaShem is always nearer to you than your soul and more distant than the farthest star. This is the message you repeat each time you say a berakhah.

The rabbis said we should search each day for a hundred reasons to say a berakhah. The berakhot remind us of the wonders of the world, from its most elemental fact—that bread can be brought forth from the earth—to its greatest marvels—rainbows, children, and the power of the human body to heal itself. We say berakhot

over comets, earthquakes, thunder, storm, and lightning, over mountains, hills, oceans, rivers, and deserts . . . over rain and over good news . . . over bad news . . . over ills that conceal good and over good things that conceal ills . . . even on beholding kings and great men, the sages of Israel, and those of the non-Jewish world (Ber. 9:2, 3, 5ff).

We also say berakhot

over fruit growing on trees . . . over wine . . . over vegetables growing on the ground . . . over bread . . . over products that do not grow on the earth [and] after meals (Ber. 6:1, 3, 6).

There are three basic types of berakhot. The **birkhot hanehenin** (בִּרְכוֹת הַנֶּהֱנִין) thank HaShem for pleasant things such as eating, drinking, smelling, and enjoying. The **birkhot hamitzvot** (בִּרְכוֹת הַמִּצְוֹת) are recited before we do a mitzvah such as putting on tefillin, lighting Shabbat candles, or studying Torah. Finally, a berakhah that celebrates our gratitude for the goodness of HaShem, the glory and wonder of the world, is called **birkat shevaḥ v'hoda'ah** (בִּרְכַּת שֶׁבַח וְהוֹדָאָה).

Taken together, all the berakhot remind us of a very important truth: There is a God who gives to you as He takes from you, who is deeply involved in your life, and whom you may not ignore.

WHY DO WE SAY BERAKHOT?

You may think of something as yours, yet it does not really belong to you. It belongs to HaShem. It may be an apple or it may be the house you live in, but it only belongs to you in the narrowest legal sense; in reality, all things belong to HaShem. A berakhah is a way of asking HaShem's permission truly to take possession of a thing, in law and in spirit. To do this, you must give thanks to the One who creates all things.

You may be doing a mitzvah such as lighting candles. Are you lighting them because they are pretty? No, the berakhah reminds you that you are lighting the candles because HaShem commands it. You may have just finished eating and feel pleasantly full. But it's not your stomach you celebrate: it's HaShem who chose you to be nourished and to grow. And for that, you must thank HaShem. Whenever we celebrate a joyous occasion, taste a new fruit for the first time, wear a new outfit, buy a car, or hear good news, we say a berakhah. In that way we weave a consciousness of the Creator through the common events of our lives.

Just as scientists learn about the world by studying and observing it, you discover the marvels of the world by celebrating them through berakhot. On the walls of many synagogues and above many an Aron HaKodesh is the inscription, "Know before Whom you stand." This inscription—which includes the word "before," *devant*—reminds you that as you daven, you are in HaShem's presence. In the same way, berakhot remind you that you are in HaShem's presence all the time. Remembering this helps you live a full Jewish life, and looking for a reason to say a hundred berakhot a day truly helps you know before Whom you stand.

Davening with kavanah means concentrating on the prayers and putting your whole self into your tefillah.

CHAPTER FOUR

EATING

ר׳ יוחנן ור׳ אלעזר דאמרי תרווייהו
כל זמן שבהמ״ק קיים
מזבח מכפר על ישראל
ועכשיו שלחנו של אדם מכפר עליו.

Rabbi Yohanan said, "So long as the Bet HaMikdash was in existence, the altar used to atone for Israel, but now a person's table atones."

(Ber. 55a)

Eating is one of life's most wonderful necessities. Everything that lives must eat. But what you choose to eat and how you choose to eat it tell a great deal about you. The Torah urges you to choose your food for the sake of higher ideals, provided for you by a higher authority.

The Torah provides very specific laws about what you are and are not permitted to eat. These regulations are called the laws of **kashrut** (כַּשְׁרוּת).

KASHRUT AND KEDUSHAH

The commandments in Leviticus concerning kashrut end with this simple but eloquent statement:

כִּי אֲנִי יהוה הַמַּעֲלֶה אֶתְכֶם מֵאֶרֶץ מִצְרַיִם לִהְיֹת לָכֶם לֵאלֹהִים
וִהְיִיתֶם קְדֹשִׁים כִּי קָדוֹשׁ אָנִי:

For I am the Lord, who brought you out of the land of Egypt to be your God: you shall be holy, for I am holy (11:45).

The word "holy," or **kadosh** (קָדוֹשׁ), means "set apart." It serves to separate those who observe the laws of kashrut from those who eat only to satisfy their appetites. HaShem places His mark on time, as with Shabbat; on language, as when you daven; on thought, as when you learn Torah. But He also places His mark on our most common everyday activity, eating. By distinguishing kosher from nonkosher,

You can keep kosher and still eat many of your favorite foods. But a product isn't kosher just because the seller says it is. You need to look for a symbol or certificate of kashrut from a reliable organization.

meat from dairy, slaughtered from killed, and Pesaḥ food from ḥametz, the Jewish people serves HaShem and keeps its integrity intact.

Setting things apart to make them special is a common activity in our lives. We regularly celebrate birthdays, anniversaries, holidays, and festivals. Viewed objectively, each of these days is nothing more than another number on a calendar. We are the ones who make these days special, by giving them a value that separates them from the rest of the year. We express this value in the way we speak about and act on each "special" day.

When the value we assign something connects it to the special relationship we have with HaShem, the value is often expressed in terms of **kedushah** (קְדֻשָּׁה, "holiness"). By observing specific rituals and dietary laws, we make things **kasher** (כָּשֵׁר, "fit" or "proper").

YOUR TABLE AND THE ALTAR

Kashrut at mealtime has always been important to Jewish rellgious life, but it assumed an even more prominent role because of the historical changes that affected the fate of the Jews around the year 70 C.E. From the year 63 B.C.E. onward, the Jews had been under the rule of the Roman Empire. The year 66 C.E. marks the beginning of a war between the Jews and the Romans that continued for seven

Friends, food, and d'var Torah recall the days of the Bet HaMikdash.

years, ending with the defeat of the Jews in 73. The most devastating defeat for the Jews during this war was the destruction of the Bet HaMikdash in 70 C.E. With the loss of the Jews' religious center, the Jewish way of life was drastically and irrevocably changed.

Without the Bet HaMikdash there was no longer a place to offer sacrifices, or **korbanot** (קָרְבָּנוֹת), or to perform the **Avodah** (עֲבוֹדָה), or Temple service, as the kohanim had done for generations. Because certain rituals were no longer possible without the Bet HaMikdash, other rituals and customs became prominent, replacing those that were lost. Verbal tefillah became more important, with prayers intended to remind the people of the Temple korbanot. Similarly, the dining table took on increased significance, as mealtimes brought memories of the Bet HaMikdash altar and the korbanot that were performed there.

Rabbi Yoḥanan said: "So long as the Bet HaMikdash was in existence, the altar used to atone for Israel, but now a person's table atones for him" (Ber. 55a). Rabbi Yoḥanan meant that although it was no longer possible to offer korbanot without the existence of the Bet HaMikdash, part of the Avodah could be done at home, when you eat. He was forging a strong link between your table and the altar. What remained was to show how you could make that connection at home.

The rabbis of the Talmud were quick to note many parallels between the Bet HaMikdash and the dining table of the Jewish home. As the altar was the central focus of the Bet HaMikdash, so the dining table became the central focus of the home. The altar and the table are both places where people consume food that comes from living things, and in both places we have a duty to remember that every living thing is created by HaShem. Like the altar in ancient times, your table is the place where you thank HaShem for the food He has provided. Because of these many similarities, it was not long before the dining table and mealtime came to assume many of the customs that had been previously associated with the Bet HaMikdash altar.

ANGELS AND HUMANS

The rabbis turned to the Torah for guidance in developing a distinctively Jewish sense of what behavior was appropriate at mealtime. This is how the Torah describes Abraham's meal with the three angels: "And he stood above them, under the tree, and they did eat" (Gen. 18:8). Puzzled by this verse, a disciple of the eighteenth-century Rabbi Zusya of Hanipol asked him if it was not strange that Scripture should say that the man stood above the angels. No, Rabbi Zusya explained, it was not strange at all. The angels are superior to man, he explained, but man is also superior to the angels. The angels are superior to man because they are pure and not part of the natural world. Man is superior to the angels because, though he is a part of

Berakhot for Mealtimes

If you are having a sit-down meal, with bread, do this:

1. Just before you sit down, wash your hands—even though you've already washed to be clean. With a cup pour a generous amount of water on each hand twice, as follows—right, right; left, left. Nothing should touch your wet hands; if something does, you must wash again. Your hands should have no rings on them; however, if a ring or wedding band is not easily removed, you may wash with it on, since it is part of you.

Now you rub your hands together and raise them somewhat. Before beginning to dry them, you recite the berakhah:

בָּרוּךְ אַתָּה, יהוה אֱלֹהֵינוּ, מֶלֶךְ הָעוֹלָם, אֲשֶׁר קִדְּשָׁנוּ בְּמִצְוֹתָיו וְצִוָּנוּ עַל נְטִילַת יָדָיִם.

Blessed are You, Lord, our God, King of the universe, who has sanctified us through His commandments and has commanded us about washing the hands.

2. Between this blessing and the blessing over the meal, you should not speak.

3. Dip the bread in salt, as salt was needed for the sacrifices on the altar, and make the **motzi** (מוֹצִיא), the berakhah over bread:

בָּרוּךְ אַתָּה, יהוה אֱלֹהֵינוּ, מֶלֶךְ הָעוֹלָם, הַמּוֹצִיא לֶחֶם מִן הָאָרֶץ.

Blessed are You, Lord, our God, King of the universe, who brings forth bread from the earth.

4. Do not speak between saying the motzi and taking the first bite of bread.

OTHER BASIC BERAKHOT

wine = **hagafen**: בּוֹרֵא פְּרִי הַגָּפֶן, " . . . who creates the fruit of the vine"

cake = **mezonot**: בּוֹרֵא מִינֵי מְזוֹנוֹת, " . . . who creates various kinds of nourishment"

water = **shehakol**: שֶׁהַכֹּל נִהְיָה בִּדְבָרוֹ, " . . . through whose Word all things were called into being"

fruit = **ha'etz**: בּוֹרֵא פְּרִי הָעֵץ, " . . . who creates the fruit of the tree"

vegetables = **ha'adamah**: בּוֹרֵא פְּרִי הָאֲדָמָה, " . . . who creates the fruit of the earth"

BERAKHOT FOR OTHER FOODS AND BEVERAGES

applesauce = shehakol

bagel = motzi

banana = ha'adamah

blintzes = mezonot

bran flakes = mezonot

calzone = mezonot as snack; motzi as full meal

chocolate = shehakol

chocolate milk = shehakol

chulent = mezonot for barley or kishke; ha'adamah for potatoes

coleslaw = ha'adamah

corn bread = mezonot as snack; motzi as full meal

custard = shehakol

doughnut = mezonot

egg salad = shehakol

eggplant = ha'adamah

fish and chips = shehakol for fish; ha'adamah for chips

french toast = motzi

granola bar = mezonot

hot dog on roll = motzi

ice cream = shehakol

kishke = mezonot

lasagne = mezonot

meat, fowl, or fish = shehakol

noodle casserole = mezonot

pasta = mezonot

peanut butter = ha'adamah

peanut butter and jelly sandwich = motzi

pickle = ha'adamah

pineapple = ha'adamah

pizza = mezonot (one slice as snack), motzi (two slices as full meal)

porridge = mezonot

raisin bran = mezonot

spaghetti and meatballs = mezonot for spaghetti; shehakol for meatballs

There is no berakhah for aspirin or other medicines and unflavored vitamins. For flavored vitamins, you say shehakol.

Source: Binyamin Forst and Aaron D. Twerski, *The Laws of Berachos* (New York: Artscroll Mesorah, 1990).

nature, he has the power to make kadosh the common, natural acts of which the angels knew nothing.

Abraham's reception of the angels illustrates another Jewish value which is closely associated with food. That value is hospitality, or **hakhnasat orḥim** (הַכְנָסַת אוֹרְחִים, "welcoming visitors"). Inviting visitors to share a meal with you is not just a matter of courtesy. Hakhnasat orḥim is an act of kedushah—a mitzvah through which we share the bounty that HaShem has provided for us. In Avot de Rabbi Nathan we read:

Abraham . . . went out and wandered about, and when he found wayfarers, he brought them to his house. . . . And not only this, but he built large inns on the roads and put food and drink within them, and all came and ate and drank and blessed HaShem (ARN [ver. I], VII, 17b.)

THE CEREMONY OF EATING

To remind us of the Bet HaMikdash and of the avodah that was performed there, a series of precise ceremonies and prayers are observed both before and after the meal. Before sitting down to eat, you pour water over your hands; this special washing is done only when your hands are already clean.

After you wash your hands, you are in an elevated state. You do not speak until you have begun eating. At the table the first words you utter are the words of the berakhah over bread, to thank HaShem for providing your food:

בָּרוּךְ אַתָּה, יהוה אֱלֹהֵינוּ, מֶלֶךְ הָעוֹלָם, הַמּוֹצִיא לֶחֶם מִן הָאָרֶץ.

Blessed are You, Lord, our God, King of the universe, who brings forth bread from the earth.

Immediately afterward, you sprinkle a little salt on a piece of bread and eat it. The salt reminds you of the salt which was put on the ancient sacrifices. The meal has begun. Enjoy it.

No meal in which bread is served is complete without saying—or **bentshing**, which is the Yiddish word for this "blessing"—the **Birkat HaMazon** (בִּרְכַּת הַמָּזוֹן), the "Grace after Meals," which is required of women and men. Three adult males form a **mezuman** (מְזֻמָּן), a quorum for public bentshing. In the Birkat HaMazon you thank HaShem for the food you have just eaten. You also thank Him for Eretz Yisrael and for Jerusalem, to which our lives are forever tied. Judaism reminds us of this connection many times each day. It is a simple truth that the Jews were able to reestablish an independent homeland in 1948 only because they had cherished Eretz Yisrael every day, at mealtimes and in their tefillot, for over 2500 years.

In the last part of the Birkat HaMazon, you ask HaShem to bless the members of your household and those sitting at your table; today, it is customary to add verses for the welfare of Jews who are oppressed. During the bentshing, as during Kiddush on Shabbat,

When baking ḥallah, we pinch off a small piece of dough and burn it in the oven. This practice commemorates the ancient gift of ḥallah to the kohanim (Num. 15:19-20).

knives are covered to remind us that no knife was permitted on the altar of the Bet HaMikdash. Knives are tools for war, and the altar was a sign of peace.

During the meal, you should try to exercise good manners. Showing good manners is more than a matter of simple etiquette; it is another way of showing respect for the table, for the act of eating, for the altar of the Bet HaMikdash, and for HaShem.

You should also try to speak some words of Torah, a **d'var Torah** (דְּבַר תּוֹרָה), at every meal. Your d'var Torah does not need to be lengthy or complicated or brilliant—just a thought that you came across or remember. The important thing is simply mentioning a word from HaShem's Torah. Just as you gain strength from the good foods that HaShem has provided, speaking words of Torah allows your mind to rise to a higher level. Rabbi Simeon said,

Just because an animal was slaughtered in a kosher way doesn't mean its meat is kosher when you buy it. The kosher butcher must remove certain blood vessels and muscles that are not kosher and must prevent the blood in the meat from drying up or congealing.

If three have eaten at a table and have spoken no words of Torah, it is as if they had eaten of sacrifices to dead idols. . . . But if three have eaten at a table and have spoken words of Torah, it is as if they had eaten at the table of the Shekhinah, God's presence . . . (Avot 3:3).

This is the ceremony of eating. When you follow this ceremony, your home becomes a sort of Bet HaMikdash, your table becomes an altar, your meal a korban, and you a servant of HaShem. What seems a minor thing—sitting down to eat—becomes a holy act of praising and serving HaShem.

LAWS OF KASHRUT

The religious practices created by the rabbis teach you the way you should eat. But even before you sit down at the table, a great deal of work has been done to make sure the food you eat has been selected and prepared in accordance with the laws of kashrut. The following are just some of the laws that will assist you in keeping kosher.

Terms of Kashrut

KASHER (כָּשֵׁר): The word "kasher" means "fit" or "proper." This term is used when speaking of the proper preparation and fitness of food. "Kasher" also refers to many religious objects, including Torah scrolls (**sifrei Torah**, סִפְרֵי תּוֹרָה), mezuzot, tefillin, and tallit.

TEREFAH (טְרֵפָה): When food is not kasher, it is terefah. The word "terefah" originally referred to an animal whose limb had been torn off by a wild beast. In Exodus 22:30 we read: "And you shall be holy to Me, therefore you shall not eat meat torn off by a wild beast in the field; you shall throw it to the dogs." In contemporary usage, terefah refers to any food not considered kasher.

NEVELAH (נְבֵלָה): "Nevelah," like "terefah," refers to food that is not kasher. The term "nevelah," however, applies specifically to a case in which the animal was not slaughtered according to the laws of kashrut. If the animal died a natural death or was killed in a violent way, it is nevelah and thus not fit for Jews to eat.

All vegetables and other plants are kosher. So are all four-footed animals that chew the cud and have a split hoof, as long as these animals are not prepared in a nonkosher way. Chickens, turkeys, ducks, geese, and other fowl that do not feed on animal carcasses are kosher. Fish that have both fins and scales are also kosher. Any animal, fowl, or fish that does not meet these standards is **terefah** (טְרֵפָה).

The Torah lists certain birds which are not kosher. Since we cannot precisely identify which birds the Torah means, we generally eat only from birds which have traditionally been considered kosher. We do not eat reptiles or insects.

Pig is not kosher, since it does not chew its cud; rabbit is not kosher because it does not have a split hoof. Many wild animals are not kosher because they are hunters or scavengers, living by destroying other lives. We do not eat shellfish of any kind, and we do not eat eel. If a kosher animal dies a natural death, it is **nevelah** (נְבֵלָה) and may not be eaten. If an otherwise kosher animal is killed by other animals, or by human beings in a way which is not kosher, then the animal becomes nevelah. Even if an animal is normally kosher and is slaughtered in a kosher way, it can become terefah if an examination reveals it was diseased. The word "terefah" really means "torn," but we have come to use it to mean anything which is not kosher, even if it is nevelah.

Even some parts of kosher animals are not kosher. For example, you are not permitted to eat the muscle along the thigh of an animal. This prohibition recalls the experience of Jacob, who wrestled all through the night with the angel. When the angel could not defeat

Jacob, it wounded the socket of Jacob's hip. Afterward, Jacob limped—but he was victorious, and his name was forever changed from Jacob to Israel.

This is why the children of Israel to this day do not eat the thigh muscle that is on the socket of the hip, since Jacob's hip socket was wrenched at the thigh muscle (Gen. 32:33).

You probably will never come into contact with this law, since kosher butchers routinely remove the muscle of the thigh. But it is important for you to know about this special law of kashrut, called **gid hanasheh** (גִּיד הַנָּשֶׁה).

Another item covered under the laws of kashrut is blood. Jewish tradition holds that blood is the life of the person. Jews do eat meat, but out of a deep and abiding respect for life, Jews never eat blood (Lev. 3:17; Deut. 12:23-25). By the process of kashering we salt the meat to remove the blood.

One of the most important laws of kashrut regards the mixing of meat and milk. This is a prohibition you will confront time and again, and about which you should be exceedingly careful. We do not mix meat and dairy products, although we are allowed to mix fish and dairy. Three times the Torah tells us, "You shall not boil the kid in the milk of its mother" (Ex. 23:19, 34:26; Deut. 14:21). The rabbis understood this threefold repetition to mean three separate prohibitions:

1. Meat and milk must not be cooked together.
2. Meat products and milk products must not be eaten at the same meal.
3. No benefit may be derived from meat which was cooked with milk, as, for example, by selling it.

In order to keep meat and milk products separate, each kosher household must own two sets of pots and pans, dishes, and silverware—one for use at dairy meals and one for use with meat. After eating dairy products, most Jews wait at least a half-hour before eating meat. If the taste of a milk product still lingers, Jews often brush their teeth or rinse their mouths before proceeding to eat meat. After eating meat, Jews wait—some for three hours, others for six, according to their family's custom—before eating dairy again.

SHEḤITAH

Under the laws of kashrut, even the slaughtering of animals is performed in a way that reflects the respect Jews have for every living thing HaShem has created.

Kosher slaughter of animals and fowl is called **sheḥitah** (שְׁחִיטָה), and the person who performs it is called a **shoḥet** (שׁוֹחֵט). The shoḥet must be a well-trained, religious Jew. He must use a knife that has been carefully sharpened, making sure there is no nick in the blade.

Kashering cooking and eating utensils for Pesaḥ in Jerusalem. Nonporous items used only for cold food may be kashered by rinsing, but most cooking utensils must be boiled before they are suitable for Passover use.

Table Manners, Jewish Style

These basic rules for eating are distilled from the Shulḥan Arukh (Oraḥ Ḥayyim, 170) and commentaries.

1. Before you eat, make sure the person serving you has eaten. This principle is called **midat ḥasidut** (מִדַּת חֲסִידוּת), "the pious way." Midat ḥasidut is especially important if the food is a gourmet delicacy or is particularly pungent or spicy, to avoid triggering any feeling of envy in the server.

2. Do not eat from a poor person's limited food supply even if he offers, unless the refusal will embarrass him. This principle is called **avak gezel** (אֲבַק גֶּזֶל), the "dust of robbery"—not robbery outright, but a hint of it.

3. Before sitting down to eat, feed the birds and animals. The Shema shows who takes precedence: "And I will provide grass in your field for your cattle, and you shall eat and be satisfied" (Deut. 11:15).

4. Practice hakhnasat orḥim by asking your parents' permission to welcome guests to your house. Hospitality is a great mitzvah. The Torah describes it often. The rabbis urge it always.

5. Before you eat, wash your hands and recite the berakhah. You are Jewish, and the food you consume is a gift from HaShem.

6. Do not follow the example of Esau by eating ravenously, like a famished beast. Gulping your food is neither attractive nor healthful. You are forbidden to harm your body, which belongs not to you but to HaShem.

7. Do not waste food—ever. Do not throw bread—even with the intention of passing it, or as a prank.

8. Do not eat in public thoroughfares where food is not meant to be eaten. This means not eating on the run, in the street, on a bus, even in a classroom or at the synagogue.

9. Eat like a mensch, a human being. Do not eat while standing. Do not eat with your hands. Do not eat in any way that offends those sharing your table. Do not pull food apart. There are some people who, on Shabbat, tear ḥallah to "break bread." But this old custom is always done with discretion and respect.

10. Do not leave the table before bentshing the berakhot after meals, the Birkat HaMazon.

11. Do not leave the table until there is some indication that the meal is over, usually signaled when the host rises.

Remember: Jews do not eat pig. Jews do not eat like pigs.

The shoḥet takes great care to keep the animals' suffering at a minimum, and the sheḥitah is performed as swiftly and painlessly as possible.

After the animal is slaughtered, the shoḥet examines it to be sure that it is not diseased. This inspection is called **bedikah** (בְּדִיקָה). If the animal was healthy, the shoḥet next removes the arteries, sinews, and certain fats from the meat and sets aside any pieces of meat which are not considered kosher.

The last step in kashering (sometimes done at home) is salting the meat, to draw out the blood. After all the blood has been removed, the salt is washed off. When salting is done properly, kosher meat will still be red, but never bloody. Meat must be washed and salted within three days of sheḥitah.

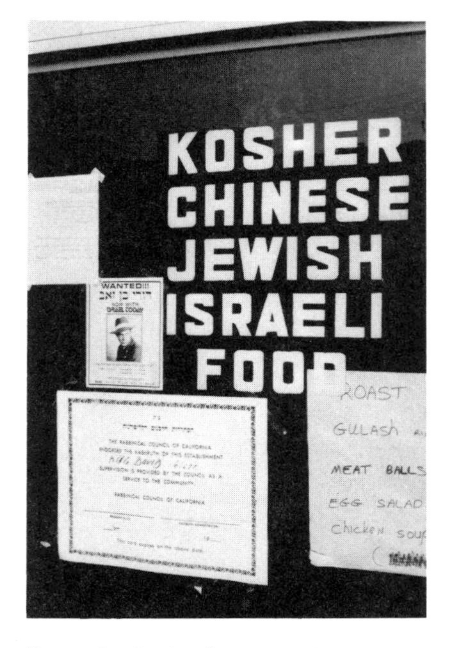

Savor the foods of many nations, but check the restaurant window for the certificate of kashrut.

KOSHER AND NONKOSHER

There is much more to know about what is and what is not kosher. The Talmud includes twenty-eight pages of discussion just on the separation of meat from milk, and there are eleven sections and sixty-two subsections on the same subject in the Shulḥan Arukh. Rabbinic authorities issue regular listings of new products reporting whether or not they are fit for use by Jews who keep kosher.

For example, a food product may contain mono- and diglycerides that derive from nonkosher animals, or rennet that comes from the stomach lining of calves not slaughtered according to halakhah. These are terefah, and even a tiny amount renders the product nonkosher.

If you're wondering how just a trace of terefah can make such a tremendous difference, consider the following true story. Dr. Louis Finkelstein, an important contemporary scholar, visited the orchestral conductor André Kostelanetz, whose wife served cookies. The rabbi refused them, explaining that he kept kosher and that a tiny ingredient in the cookies would render them terefah. The conductor asked him what a tiny speck of terefah could possibly do to his soul. The rabbi responded by asking what the final crescendo of Beethoven's Fifth Symphony would sound like if the conductor left out just one bar. Kostelanetz smiled knowingly: it would ruin the entire symphony!

Older products are tested regularly to check whether they continue to be produced in a kosher way. There are many organizations in the United States, Israel, Europe, and around the world that research the kashrut of the food products we buy. You should learn to look for certain symbols of these organizations on the labels in your local supermarket. One common, reliable symbol certifying that a food is kosher is Ⓤ, which stands for Union of Orthodox Jewish Congregations. The simple K symbol, however, can be affixed by anyone and is not sufficient assurance that the product is, in fact, kosher.

Like the kosher items sold in supermarkets, restaurants that offer kosher food to the public are also inspected and certified. When eating away from home, you should always eat in a place where kosher food is available. If you do find yourself at the home of a friend who doesn't keep kosher, or in a nonkosher restaurant, you can generally eat uncooked fruits and vegetables, and many candies and soft drinks are acceptable. However, you need to make sure that not only the ingredients in the food but also the dishes and silverware with which they are served comply with the laws of kashrut; to avoid this problem, some Jews request paper plates and disposable utensils. You should consult your rabbi for further guidance on this important matter.

TZA'AR BA'ALEI ḤAYYIM

One of the principles underlying the laws of kashrut is love and respect for life. The Talmud tells us that before we sit down to our table to eat, we must first feed any animals we own. Jewish law requires many things of us in order to prevent **tza'ar ba'alei ḥayyim** (צַעַר בַּעֲלֵי חַיִּים), "cruelty to living things." Three times the Torah commands us not to cook a kid in its mother's milk, and this reminds us that even in cooking we should try to be sensitive to the life of the animal.

In another passage we read:

> **When an ox or a sheep or a goat is born, it shall stay seven days with its mother, and from the eighth day on it shall be acceptable as an offering to the Lord. However, no animal from the herd or from the flock shall be slaughtered on the same day with its young (Lev. 22:27-28).**

The rabbis noted that the ban on killing the young on the same day as its mother is a sign of mercy. Otherwise, it might accidentally

Eating is one of life's great pleasures. When you add berakhot, songs, and divrei Torah to a meal, you make eating even more enjoyable.

We say the berakhot ha'etz and ha'adamah to thank HaShem for creating fruits and vegetables.

happen that the young would be killed first and the mother would be forced to watch her offspring die. Additionally, this prohibition serves to make us more compassionate, as though telling us: you may use animals for food and for your survival, but you must still remember that you are taking the life of a living being.

THE JOY OF EATING

Despite all the laws and all the elaborate preparation, kashrut does not rob the Jewish family of pleasure in eating. Gefilte fish, chicken soup, bagels, chulent, kugel, knishes, and dozens of other delicious foods have become traditional items at Jewish tables. Keeping kosher does not mean giving up fine foods; on the contrary, many modern Jewish cooks produce gourmet meals in strictly kosher kitchens. In addition, the ceremony of eating adds its own kind of flavor to the food. This is even more true on Shabbat and the holidays, when you add songs and divrei Torah to the meal, making the eating process even more beautiful.

The Talmud tells of a time when Rabbi Joshua ben Hananiah invited the emperor of Rome to dine with his family on Shabbat:

> The emperor asked [Joshua], "What gives your Sabbath meat such an aroma?" [Joshua] replied, "We have a spice called Shabbat which is put in the cooking of the meat, and this gives the aroma." The emperor said, "Give me some of

Substance Use and Abuse

The laws of kashrut deal with foods prepared according to halakhic standards. But not all foods that meet religious standards promote good health. It is your responsibility to take care of your body and soul by eating foods that are healthy as well as kosher.

Some other substances that people introduce into their bodies are undeniably toxic and ultimately harmful. In a strict sense, these do not violate the laws of kashrut. But that does not mean we are permitted to use them. Judaism teaches that we are forbidden to injure our bodies. Your body belongs to HaShem. You have no right to destroy or deface HaShem's property.

SMOKING. Before medical evidence clearly established the health risks associated with smoking, many great rabbis sought to permit smoking by citing Psalm 116: "The Lord preserves the simple." These rabbis taught that since we are unsure of smoking's long-term effects, we may leave the matter to HaShem.

Today, however, we are no longer "simple." The United States government and every major medical institution, without exception, have condemned smoking as a threat to health. We now understand that using tobacco products contradicts the teaching that forbids us to injure our bodies. If you don't smoke, don't start—and if you do smoke, stop. Eating terefah is bad. Inhaling smoke—or causing others to inhale it—is irresponsible.

When you smoke, use illegal drugs, or abuse alcohol, you not only harm yourself—you also destroy what properly belongs to HaShem.

DRUGS. Using illegal drugs of any kind is the worst violation of the Torah's mandate to care for the body. In addition to destroying both body and mind, drug addiction causes us to lose control over our lives and violate the laws of the land, When you take drugs, you commit treason to the Jewish family and the Jewish people.

ALCOHOL. Jews do drink wine for sacred purposes: at Kiddush and Havdalah on Shabbat, at the Passover seder, at weddings, at a circumcision, and (even without Kiddush) on Purim. Often, elderly Jews drink a shot of schnapps after weekday morning services. Wine, like bread, is a special food for which we give special thanks to HaShem.

Even though they drank, Jews of prior generations rarely got drunk. This is because their drinking was associated with religious observance, and because drinking more than a moderate amount of alcohol was severely condemned by others. Today, on the other hand, alcohol is a substance very often abused, by Jews as well as non-Jews.

Excessive alcohol consumption, especially at an early age, leads easily to addiction. It harms your body and clouds your mind. It destroys families and innocent people. Noah was faulted for getting drunk after the flood; Lot got drunk and sinned severely. A kohen who is drunk is not authorized to give the priestly blessings. A Jew who is under the influence of liquor should not daven.

A sip of wine to wish a mazel tov is *l'ḥayyim*, a gift of life. Alcohol abuse is *l'mavet*, a toast to death.

this spice." Joshua answered, "For those who keep the Sabbath, the spice works; for those who do not keep the Sabbath, the spice does not work" (Shab. 119a).

KASHRUT: A JEWISH DISCIPLINE

The laws of kashrut are more than laws of eating. Practicing kashrut ties us to the generations of the past and links us to Jews throughout the world. Kashrut distinguishes you as Jewish and shows that you take pride in your Jewishness. Its practices are an outward sign that you have accepted the covenant. Although at times it may be difficult to keep kosher—especially when you are not at home—the effort is amply rewarded.

Historically, the laws of kashrut have proved helpful to Jews in numerous ways. In many times and places, taking a simple meal could prove harmful to one's health. This was rarely true in the Jewish home. The careful inspection of meat by the shoḥet, the separation of meat from milk, and the avoidance of forbidden foods (especially pork) had the added benefit of being healthful. Through the ages, one of the side-benefits of kashrut has been that Jews have suffered less from food poisoning and related diseases because of the care that kashrut required.

Finally, the laws of kashrut have proved helpful to the Jews in a very personal and intimate way. Through the centuries, the laws of kashrut have served to protect the Jewish family and its unity. Most Jews took their meals at home—or in the house of a friend or neighbor who was known to be equally observant. This meant that Jewish families spent much time together—eating, talking, bentshing, and sharing their stories and Torah-talk around the dining table. Mealtimes became family times. Each meal became a miniature religious event, elevating the mundane act of eating to an exalted act of celebration.

CHAPTER FIVE

HOME

יוֹסֵי בֶּן יוֹעֶזֶר אוֹמֵר:
יְהִי בֵיתְךָ בֵּית וַעַד לַחֲכָמִים.

Yose ben Yoezer of Zeredah said, "Let your house be a meeting place for the wise. . . ."
(Avot 1:4)

When we think of HaShem, the first place we might think of is the synagogue, or bet knesset. The bet knesset is also called **mikdash me'at** (מִקְדָּשׁ מְעַט), the "small sanctuary." Public Shabbat services are conducted there, as are the services for weekdays and Yom Tov. So perhaps we feel the presence of HaShem most strongly when we are at the bet knesset, surrounded by the entire community. But if the bet knesset is where we display our public relationship with HaShem, it is at home, in the privacy of our family, that we often share our most intimate and personal experiences with Him.

The bet knesset may be the center of community activity, but the home is in most respects the focal point of Jewish life. Before and after every meal at home you say berakhot. Each night before retiring you say the Shema. You light candles and recite the Kiddush to begin every Shabbat evening, and you recite Havdalah to acknowledge the Sabbath's end. The Passover seder and the lighting of the Ḥanukkah menorah are also observed at home. Taken together, these and many other mitzvot create a heightened awareness of HaShem. They turn a household into a Jewish home, a **bayit ne'eman** (בַּיִת נֶאֱמָן).

In Psalm 127 it is written:

Unless the Lord builds the house, its builders labor in vain on it. . . .

In the pages that follow, we will examine the various ways that HaShem has "built" the house we live in, and how we may take an active role in building that house with Him.

MEZUZAH

The first symbol you meet upon entering a Jewish home is the **mezuzah** (מְזוּזָה). A mezuzah hangs on the outside doorpost; traditional Jewish homes have a mezuzah on the doorpost leading

A 98-year-old cantor led the model seder at this special Jewish home—the Daughters of Jacob Geriatric Center in New York City.

Almost every Jewish home has a pair of candlesticks to be used on Shabbat and Yom Tov evenings. Some households light an additional Shabbat candle for each child in the family.

The House of Jacob: A Glossary

The twentieth-century French philosopher Jacques Maritain spoke of the Jewish people not as a race, a nationality, or a people, but as a "house." In this sense, Jews are one family, members of **Bet Ya'akov** (בֵּית יַעֲקֹב), the "House of Jacob."

In a house we find disparate elements—people, books, opinions, loyalties, observances, customs, habits—all united under one roof. Similarly, Bet Ya'akov includes many different kinds of people: gifted and ordinary, rich and poor, righteous and renegade, religiously observant and indifferent. Some members of Bet Ya'akov are born Jews, related by blood; others are converts, related by conviction. But all those who dwell in the House of Jacob are united under one roof—HaShem.

Ideas of "house" and "home" permeate the Hebrew language and Jewish thinking. This list of some Hebrew terms that start with "bet" and "bayit" shows just how pervasive these ideas are.

RELIGIOUS TERMS

bayit ne'eman (בַּיִת נֶאֱמָן): literally, "faithful house"; an observant Jewish household.

bet Aharon (בֵּית אַהֲרֹן): the house of Aaron; the kohanim, descendants of Aaron, the High Priest.

Bet HaMikdash (בֵּית הַמִּקְדָּשׁ): the Temple of Jerusalem.

bet ḥayyim (בֵּית חַיִּים): literally, "house of life"; a graveyard or cemetery.

into nearly every room in the house. Because the mezuzah is the symbol most closely associated with the home, it is important for us to examine the ways the mezuzah reflects our most deeply held Jewish values and traditions.

Although the Hebrew word מְזוּזָה literally means "doorpost," the word "mezuzah" as it is popularly used refers to a small parchment scroll enclosed in a case or shell. The mezuzah case may be made of any durable material—wood, silver, gold, acrylic, even plastic wrap. Since this entire object is placed on the doorpost, we use the word "mezuzah" to mean either the parchment or the parchment and the case together.

The Talmud tells us that the mezuzah should be attached to the right-hand doorpost:

For it is written, "And you shall write them upon the doorposts of your house *[beitekha]*," which means "the way you enter *[bi'atkha]* your house," for when a person lifts a foot in order to go somewhere, it is the right foot which is lifted first (Men. 34a).

Bet Hillel (בֵּית הִלֵּל): the School of Hillel, a rabbi who lived in the first century B.C.E.

bet knesset (בֵּית כְּנֶסֶת): literally, "house of meeting"; the synagogue.

bet Levi (בֵּית לֵוִי): the house of Levi; the Levites who served at the Bet HaMikdash.

bet midrash (בֵּית מִדְרָשׁ): a house of learning and Talmud study; a Torah academy which was also used for public prayer.

Bet Shammai (בֵּית שַׁמַּאי): the School of Shammai, a rabbi who lived at about the same time as Hillel and often disagreed with him on halakhic matters.

Bet Ya'akov (בֵּית יַעֲקֹב): the House of Jacob; the people of Israel. Often used to refer to Jewish women as a collective.

Bet Yisrael (בֵּית יִשְׂרָאֵל): the House of Israel; the Jewish people.

INSTITUTIONS

bet din (בֵּית דִּין): Jewish court of law; the rabbinical court in which three rabbis serve as arbiters and judges in deciding legal matters.

bet ḥolim (בֵּית חוֹלִים): hospital.

bet sefer (בֵּית סֵפֶר): literally, "house of book"; a school.

bet sohar (בֵּית סוֹהַר): prison.

The commandment regarding the mezuzah is found in the familiar words of the Shema: "And these words which I command you this day . . . you shall write them on the doorposts of your house and on your gates" (Deut. 6:6-9; *see also* Deut. 11:20). The parchment scroll inside the mezuzah case contains two paragraphs of the Shema. The first begins "Hear, O Israel . . ." (Deut. 6:4-9), and the second begins, "If you will carefully obey My commandments . . ." (Deut. 11:13-21).

The paragraphs are copied by a scribe, or **sofer** (סוֹפֵר), in the special Hebrew lettering that is called Torah script. The small piece of parchment, known as the **klaf** (קְלָף), must come from the hide of a kosher animal. The klaf is rolled starting from the end of the first sentence of the Shema—the word **eḥad** (אֶחָד, "one")—to its beginning—the word **shema** (שְׁמַע, "hear")—so that the latter is on top. On the outside of the klaf, where it can be seen, the sofer writes the word שדי, one of HaShem's names. The three letters of שדי stand for the phrase **Shomer daltot Yisrael** (שׁוֹמֵר דַּלְתוֹת יִשְׂרָאֵל), which

All of us are commanded—and permitted—to affix the mezuzah. Before fastening the mezuzah to the doorpost you say:

בָּרוּךְ אַתָּה, יהוה אֱלֹהֵינוּ, מֶלֶךְ
הָעוֹלָם, אֲשֶׁר קִדְּשָׁנוּ בְּמִצְוֹתָיו,
וְצִוָּנוּ לִקְבֹּעַ מְזוּזָה.

Blessed are You, Lord, our God, King of the universe, who has sanctified us through His commandments and has commanded us to affix the mezuzah.

calls HaShem the "Guardian of the doors of Israel" (Kol Bo 90, 101:4). Once the klaf is rolled, it is placed in the mezuzah case to be fastened to the doorpost.

ORIGINS AND MEANING

The mezuzah reminds us of the events in Exodus. Just before the tenth plague, HaShem instructed Moses to have the people of Israel offer a sacrifice of lambs. The Israelites were then told to place some of the lambs' blood on the doorposts of their homes.

> For that night I will go through the land of Egypt and strike down every first-born in the land of Egypt, both man and beast. . . . And the blood on the houses where you are staying shall be a sign for you: when I see the blood I will pass over you, so that no plague will destroy you when I strike the land of Egypt (Ex. 12:12-13).

The blood marked on the doorposts of Jewish homes signaled the Angel of Death to pass over these homes during the night of the tenth plague. From this event came the idea that the mezuzah "guards" the doors of the Jewish home.

Onkelos, a second-century convert to Judaism who translated the Bible into Aramaic, described the power of the mezuzah this way. When Roman soldiers asked him to explain the strange symbol on his door, Onkelos replied that unlike a king of flesh and blood, "In the case of the Holy One, the Blessed, His servants dwell on the inside, while He watches over them from the outside" (A.Z. 11a). Rabbi Joseph Karo, author of the Shulḥan Arukh, also noted the protective power of the mezuzah. He remarked that while other mitzvot are held to shield you while you are doing the mitzvah, the mezuzah protects you even when you are not mindful of it.

For thousands of years, a mezuzah on the doorpost of a house has meant that the family living inside is Jewish. The mezuzah also reminds us that HaShem is everywhere, "when you stay at home and when you are away" (Deut. 6:7). According to a popular custom, when leaving or entering the house, Jews "kiss" the mezuzah by first touching the mezuzah case and then kissing their fingertips. This gesture of affection is a way of bringing the mezuzah close to us. Kissing the mezuzah as you leave home reminds you that HaShem is with you in the world outside; kissing it as you enter the house reminds you that HaShem is also inside, present wherever you are. Even when you are alone in the house, a mezuzah on the doorpost of each room reminds you that HaShem is always with you.

MOVING THE MEZUZAH: A CASE STUDY

Deciding whether to leave the mezuzah on the outside of a house when you move depends on who is moving into the house after you. If the people who bought your house are Jewish, you usually leave the mezuzah as a way of welcoming them: you wouldn't want to deprive them of HaShem's protection in their new home. But if the people moving in are not Jewish, you remove the mezuzah, since it is not a mitzvah to them.

Suppose the non-Jew who is about to move in says, "Please leave the mezuzah. It has brought you luck, and it may bring me luck." Can you leave the mezuzah? The answer is no. The mezuzah is sacred to the Jews. It is not a good luck charm. It is a reminder of the Oneness of HaShem.

This series of questions and answers teaches us something important about the mezuzah. The mezuzah is not an amulet, or good luck charm. Many Jews wear a miniature mezuzah on a chain around their necks. If you think of it as a piece of jewelry, like a Magen David or a charm in the shape of the two tablets of the Ten Commandments, the custom is acceptable. If you wear it to show the world that you are Jewish, that is also a fine idea. But you are forbidden to wear a true mezuzah with a kosher klaf around your neck. A person is not a doorpost. You should also refrain from wearing a mezuzah around your neck if your idea by wearing the mezuzah is to get good luck. As Rambam wrote, those who think of the mezuzah as a lucky charm

> not only fail to fulfill the mitzvah [of mezuzah] itself, but also have taken a great mitzvah, involving the Oneness of HaShem and the reminder to love HaShem and worship HaShem, and treat it as though it were an amulet designed to benefit them personally (M.T., Sefer Ahava, Hilkhot Mezuzah 5:4).

HANGING THE MEZUZAH

As soon as you move into a new home, you should hang mezuzot on its doorposts. In Eretz Yisrael this must be done at once; outside the Holy Land, however, some hold that in rented properties it may be done up to thirty days later. Perhaps one may infer from this difference that living in a dwelling in Eretz Yisrael is the preferred ideal of Torah. We hang the mezuzah elsewhere only hesitatingly.

A mezuzah must be hung on every doorpost which leads into a permanent room that people ordinarily use. We do not hang a mezuzah on a sukkah, since it is not a permanent dwelling, and we do not hang a mezuzah on a closet, bathroom, or toilet door.

The mezuzah may be put on the doorpost by anyone old enough to understand the meaning of the mitzvah. First, you recite the berakhah:

בָּרוּךְ אַתָּה, יהוה אֱלֹהֵינוּ, מֶלֶךְ הָעוֹלָם, אֲשֶׁר קִדְּשָׁנוּ בְּמִצְוֹתָיו,
וְצִוָּנוּ לִקְבֹּעַ מְזוּזָה.

Blessed are You, Lord, our God, King of the universe, who has sanctified us through His commandments and has commanded us to affix the mezuzah.

If you hang all the mezuzot in your house at one time, one after another, you recite the berakhah only once, before hanging the first mezuzah.

Once the berakhah is said, you face the door as if you were entering it and nail, screw, or glue the mezuzah on the right-hand post. The mezuzah should be hung at least two-thirds of the way up the doorpost, and at least one hand's measure from the very top. If the doorway leads into a child's room, the mezuzah should be placed, if possible, within easy reach of the child. If the doorpost is very wide, the mezuzah should be positioned within three or four inches from the outside. The mezuzah should be hung with its top tilted toward the inside and its bottom tilted out. If the doorpost is very narrow, the mezuzah can be hung vertically, straight up and down.

Why is the mezuzah hung in a slanted position? Rashi taught that the mezuzah should be hung in a vertical position, its top pointing to heaven. But Rashi's grandson, Rabbenu Tam, taught that the mezuzah should be hung horizontally, its top facing the inside of the house. Both Rashi and Rabbenu Tam were great teachers, and both had good halakhic reasons for their idea of which way the mezuzah should be hung. Since we cannot decide between them solely on the basis of the arguments they made, and since we Jews are expected to show respect for our teachers, we found a better way. The main tradition of the Ashkenazim is to hang the mezuzah diagonally, so that it is neither horizontal (which Rashi could not accept) nor vertical (which Rabbenu Tam rejected).

This silver besamim box, made in sixteenth-century Germany, is an elegant example of hiddur mitzvah.

OTHER JEWISH SYMBOLS

The mezuzah may be the most prominent sign of a bayit ne'eman, but many other important symbols mark a Jewish household. Since these objects are used in performing mitzvot, they should be treated with special attention and respect.

Almost all Jewish families have a pair of candlesticks to be used on Shabbat and Yom Tov evenings. Some Shabbat candlesticks have been passed down in the family from one generation to the next. Your family's candlesticks may be very old, reminding you of family members who are no longer living.

For Shabbat and Yom Tov, you will also find a special Kiddush cup used in reciting the blessings over wine. For ḥallah there may be a woven cloth, or ḥallah cover, to place over the loaves. Many families have a special knife, used only to cut the ḥallah, and a ḥallah plate, used only to place beneath the loaves, over which the ḥallah cover is draped.

In addition, your family should have a special set of objects for **Havdalah** (הַבְדָּלָה), the ceremony separating Shabbat and Yom Tov from the other days of the week. The Havdalah set usually includes a candlestick designed to hold the braided Havdalah candle, a Kiddush cup, and a box for fragrant spices, or **besamim** (בְּשָׂמִים). In most Jewish homes you will find a candelabra with nine branches, called a **menorah** (מְנוֹרָה). The nine-branched menorah is used for lighting the candles on the eight nights of Ḥanukkah, with one candle used to light the others.

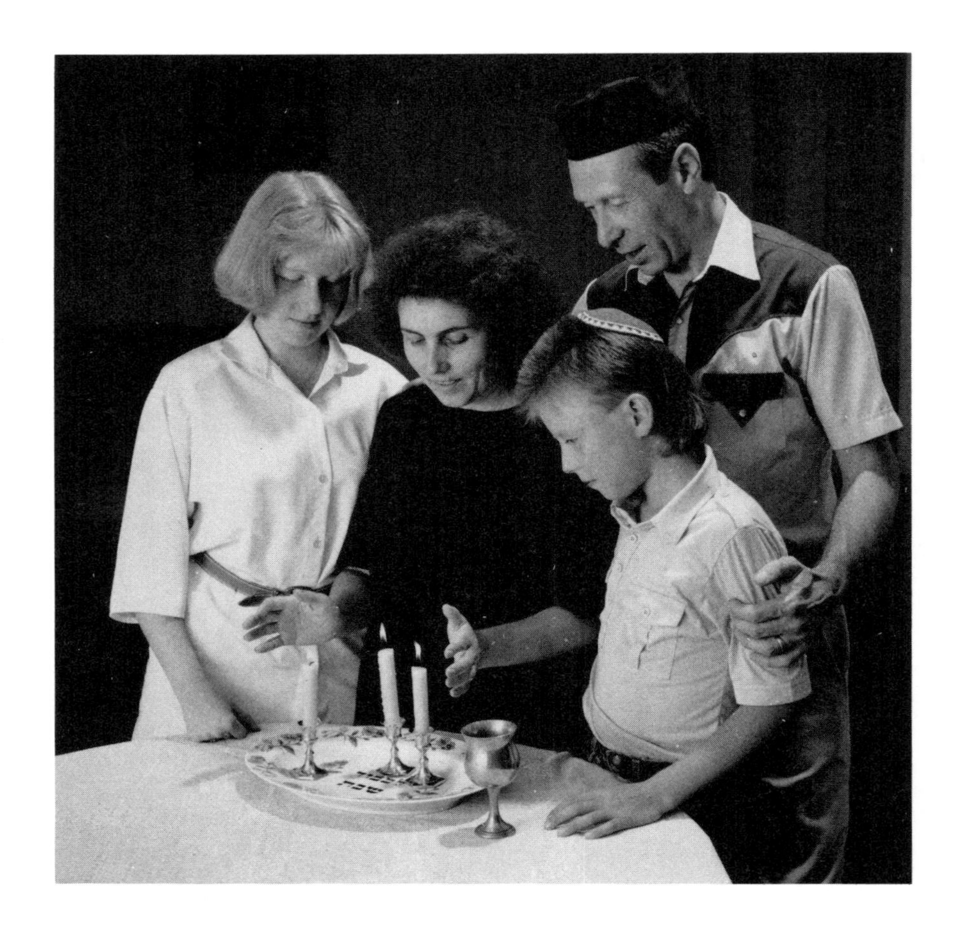

Candle-lighting was especially meaningful for this family of Russian Jews, shown celebrating Shabbat for the first time in their new home—the United States.

Your family may have both a seder plate, used during the Passover meal to hold the symbols of Pesaḥ, and another special plate for the Passover matzah. Many Jews also own a special box used once a year on the festival of Sukkot to hold the **etrog** (אֶתְרוֹג), or citron.

A charity box, or **pushka**, was found in all Jewish homes before tzedakah was given by check. The mother of the house put coins in the pushka before lighting the Shabbat candles and whenever something good happened to the family. Money was also placed in the pushka in moments of family trouble and sadness—for example, before a family member went in for surgery. It is an important custom before daily morning davening to make a small contribution to the tzedakah box.

A pewter seder plate, crafted in Germany during the eighteenth century.

BOOKS

In addition to the Jewish objects that fill your home, there are probably many Jewish books on your family's bookshelves. Almost every Jewish home has a copy of the Hebrew Bible, or **Tanakh** (תַּנַ"ךְ), and a copy of the siddur. Your family probably has books in Hebrew or English that teach the meaning of Judaism. In many homes you can find a set of the Talmud, also known by the acronym **SHAS** (שַׁ"ס), which stands for **Shishah Sedarim** (שִׁשָּׁה סְדָרִים), the six orders of the Mishnah. Your household may well own a copy of the Shulḥan Arukh; a work by Rambam, such as the Mishneh Torah; and a Jewish encyclopedia.

In the kitchen you may find a guide to kashrut or a Jewish cookbook which explains the best ways of keeping a kosher home. There may be a Jewish songbook at the piano, and books about Jewish history in the study, along with books about Israel and collections of Jewish stories and legends. Jewish magazines and newspapers probably arrive regularly. Taken together, all these books and periodicals form a little Jewish library, making your home a place for Jewish learning.

We use these Jewish books just as we use the other Jewish objects in our homes—to fulfill the mitzvot. The mitzvah of study is a daily requirement. The Mishnah says:

These are the things of which the fruits are enjoyed in this world while the capital remains for the world to come: honoring parents, kindness, bringing peace between people, and also the study of Torah, which is equal to them all (Pe'ah 1:1).

Books that teach us about HaShem's world deserve respect. The quality of the books you own—and how you treat them—is a reflection of the quality of your mind. If your personal library consists solely of books about sports, pets, hobbies, and romances, that tells the world the kind of mind you have. But if you read and treasure books about Torah and values and history, your library speaks volumes about your own love of learning.

This brass charity box, or pushka, was made in Europe more than 100 years ago. It provides a beautiful opportunity to fulfill the mitzvah of tzedakah by giving to those in need.

SH'LOM BAYIT

The special feeling that marks a home as Jewish is called **sh'lom bayit** (שְׁלוֹם בַּיִת). You know both these words. Shalom means "peace" or "unity," and bayit means "house." Together, they make a phrase we might call "family harmony," although there really is no exact English equivalent. Sh'lom bayit is an attitude, a state of mind—the feeling we get when everyone in the family is at peace with everyone else in the family. When your whole family feels together as one, then the world seems a better place and home has a new meaning. That is sh'lom bayit.

Rabbi Simeon ben Gamaliel said: When a person makes peace in his house, Torah accounts it as if he made peace for every single Israelite in Israel; when a person brings jealousy and strife into his house, [the Torah accounts it] as if he brought them among all Israel (ARN 28).

A famous story from the Midrash tells us just how important sh'lom bayit is.

Rabban Gamaliel gave his daughter in marriage. "Father," she said, "give me your blessing." He said to her: "May you never return to live in my home."

Recent Halakhic Authorities

In addition to the Jewish books mentioned in this chapter and in Chapter 1 (*see* "Major Halakhic Authorities"), you may also wish to learn about works by this selected list of more recent halakhic authorities.

REB ḤAYYIM BRISKER: Rabbi Ḥayyim Soloveitchik of Brisk (Brest-Litovsk) was born in 1853 and died in 1918. A rare genius from a family of geniuses, the Brisker rabbi innovated the analytical approach to Talmud study. His knowledge was boundless, his logic profound—and his generosity was legendary.

THE ḤAFETZ ḤAYYIM: Rabbi Israel Meir HaKohen Kagan (1838-1933) is named for his first major work, *Ḥafetz Ḥayyim* ("He Who Desires Life"), written about the laws of gossip and slander. His influence was considerable, not only because of his brilliance but also because of his total, uncompromising integrity. His greatest work is the *Mishnah Berurah* (see Chapter 1).

THE ḤAZON ISH: Rabbi Avraham Yeshayahu Karelitz was born in 1878 in Eastern Europe and died in 1953 in Israel, where he spent his last twenty years. The name *Ḥazon Ish* derives from the title of his first published work, a commentary on the Shulḥan Arukh. His profound mind ranged over an immense area of Jewish law, and he was considered the final authority, **posek aḥaron** (פּוֹסֵק אַחֲרוֹן), of his time. His greatest contribution was his mastery of laws relating to Eretz Yisrael, for which he studied mathematics and astronomy.

RAV KOOK: Rabbi Abraham Isaac Kook was born in Latvia in 1865 and rose to become the first Ashkenazi chief rabbi of modern Palestine. A lifelong lover of Eretz Yisrael and of his fellow Jews, he built bridges between Orthodox and secular Zionist pioneers. He was a master Talmudic scholar, a poet, a kabbalist, and an educational reformer who founded a famous yeshiva in Jerusalem. He believed that the return to Israel would be the beginning of spiritual renewal and redemption for the Jewish people. He died in Palestine in 1935.

THE RAV: Rabbi Joseph Soloveitchik, the grandson of Reb Ḥayyim Brisker, was born in 1903 and died in 1993. He was one of the most brilliant Jewish scholars of this century, combining the profound scholarship of Brisk with vast secular knowledge; he earned a Ph.D. in philosophy from Berlin University in 1931. He was Professor of Talmud at Yeshiva University and the master teacher of thousands of American rabbis.

THE REBBE: All Ḥasidim have a rebbe, but Menachem Mendel Schneerson, the Grand Rabbi of Lubavitch Ḥasidim, is known as *the* Rebbe. Born in Russia in 1902, he came to New York in 1940 and succeeded to the leadership of Lubavitch (also called Ḥabad) in 1951. The Rebbe is a renowned scholar, and he teaches and writes Torah every day. His many followers aggressively seek to persuade nonobservant Jews to return to HaShem and His Torah via the route of Lubavitch.

REB MOSHE: Rabbi Moses Feinstein was born in Russia in 1895 and died in New York in 1986. He was a man of prodigious knowledge and great insight and kindness. He was known as the great authority, or **posek gadol**, of the second half of the twentieth century. His many volumes of responsa, *Iggerot Moshe*, answer an enormous number of questions of the widest variety and contain many landmark decisions.

THE EMEK HALAKHAH: Rabbi Yehoshua Baumol was born in Poland in 1880 and died in New York in 1948. He was a man of great erudition and profound compassion. The collection of responsa for which he is named, *Emek Halakhah*, is renowned for its pioneering application of Jewish law to contemporary situations, especially to modern technological issues such as the lie detector.

An artist and her granddaughter share the joy of companionship at a California home for the aging. Many Jewish homes for the elderly provide kosher food, Shabbat services, and Jewish cultural events for those who live there.

"You have cursed me!" she exclaimed. "I have blessed you," he replied. "If you live at peace in your new home, you will not return here" (Gen. R. 26:4)

Of course, perfect sh'lom bayit rarely happens; it is something we constantly have to work at. Yet it is possible for us to achieve it. And even if we do not finally achieve it, working toward sh'lom bayit remains extremely important. More than the symbols of Judaism or the Jewish books on the shelf, it is the unity of the Jewish family—sh'lom bayit—which makes a Jewish home.

BET YISRAEL

While striving for sh'lom bayit in our own households, each of us also has a responsibility to extend that feeling throughout **Bet Yisrael** (בֵּית יִשְׂרָאֵל), the "House of Israel." In many homes the pushka is a reminder of our obligation to be generous with our wealth. But you don't need to be wealthy to help others in the community. All members of Bet Yisrael have a responsibility to extend sh'lom bayit to the entire community by clothing, feeding, and housing those in need of help. Today we have a special obligation to address the plight of the many Jewish homeless. Every member of Bet Yisrael deserves a bayit.

Every Jewish community contains many different kinds of "homes." There may be a Jewish hospital, a temporary home for Jews who are ill. There may be a home for the Jewish aged, or apartments set aside for poorer Jews who need reasonably priced housing. There may be homes for Jews in various kinds of distress: Jews suffering from chronic diseases; Jewish women forced to flee from husbands who were physically abusive; battered Jewish children; Jewish immigrants newly arrived from countries where they were oppressed. Other special homes, called hospices, provide care for Jews who are terminally ill. Prisons also contain Jews who need your attention.

All of these are Jewish homes, and all of them need sh'lom bayit. We support them not only by giving tzedakah (although that remains important), but also through the work of our hands.

It is written, "Seek peace and pursue it" (Ps. 34:15). The Law does not order you to run after, or pursue, the other mitzvot, only to fulfill them when the appropriate occasion arrives. . . . But peace you must seek in your own place, and also run after it to another (Num. R., Ḥukkat, 19:27).

Rabbi Simeon ben Elazar said: "If a man sits in his place and keeps silent, how can he pursue peace between man and man in Israel? Let him leave his place and roam about in the world, and pursue peace in Israel. Seek peace in your own home, and pursue it to another place" (ARN 12).

Just as we are obliged to bring sh'lom bayit to our own homes, so we are required to bring shalom to Bet Yisrael.

Shabbat observance at another special Jewish home: a halfway house for Jewish convicts.

CHAPTER SIX

TORAH

לֹא־יָמוּשׁ סֵפֶר הַתּוֹרָה הַזֶּה מִפִּיךָ.

This Torah shall not depart from your lips. . . .

(Joshua 1:8)

During the Middle Ages, a story was told of a Jewish scholar who took a long journey on a merchant ship. To pass the time, the merchants would talk about spices, satins, and silks. At last, they turned to the Jewish scholar and asked, "What goods do you trade?" He replied, "I carry all my goods with me." The merchants all laughed at him. After all, how much merchandise could one man possibly carry? But the scholar insisted, "My goods are the best."

The next day, the ship was attacked by pirates, who stole all the merchants' expensive goods. When the merchants reached port, they had nothing to sell.

That evening, the merchants saw the scholar enter the bet midrash. They were amazed when he came out—followed by people offering him food and housing, even money to live on.

"Didn't I tell you?" the Jewish scholar said to the merchants. "My goods really are the best. Everything you had was lost, but my goods can never be taken away from me. My merchandise is called Torah! And Torah is the best *s'ḥorah* [merchandise]!"

Of course, this is just a legend, but there is much truth in it. For a Jew, Torah is the greatest treasure. Our people has always placed the value of Torah study above rubies, emeralds, and diamonds. Our enemies might destroy our homes and synagogues, they might even expel us from the country, but they could never destroy our most priceless treasure. It goes where we go—it is in our minds and hearts. This is the Torah which HaShem gave us at Sinai.

THE MEANING OF TORAH

You can see how precious this treasure is by the special way we use the word **Torah** (תּוֹרָה). In its very simplest meaning, Torah stands for the first five books of the Bible. These five books are collectively known as **Ḥumash** (חוּמָּשׁ), a word that comes from the Hebrew word for the number five, **ḥamesh** (חָמֵשׁ).

Study is both a daily responsibility and a lifelong pursuit. Above, members of an adult Jewish discussion group in Los Angeles; below, a student at a Hebrew day school in New York City.

A Page of Ḥumash

1 ḤUMASH, the "five," referring to the Five Books of Moses.

2 TARGUM ONKELOS, the Aramaic translation made in the second century C.E. by Onkelos ben Kalonymos, a convert to Judaism.

3 RASHI, the most famous of all commentators on Ḥumash. The name **Rashi** is an acronym for **Ra**bbi **Sh**lomo ben **I**saac (1040-1105).

4 IBN EZRA, the Spanish rabbi Abraham ibn Ezra (1089-1164), who was also a poet, astronomer, and physician. His commentary relies on grammar and etymology to explain the literal meaning of the text.

רשי　　שמות יג בא　　אבן עזרא　　לח

[illegible]

לך הזכרים ליהוה: יג וכל פטר חמר תפדה בשה ואם לא תפדה וערפתו וכל בכור אדם בבניך תפדה: יד והיה כי ישאלך בנך מחר לאמר מה זאת ואמרת אליו בחזק יד הוציאנו יהוה ממצרים מבית עבדים: טו ויהי כי הקשה פרעה לשלחנו ויהרג יהוה כל בכור בארץ מצרים מבכר אדם ועד בכור בהמה על כן אני זבח ליהוה כל פטר רחם הזכרים וכל בכור בני אפדה: טז והיה לאות על ידכה ולטוטפת בין עיניך כי בחזק יד הוציאנו יהוה ממצרים: ס ס ס

ק״ח ימנח סימן

דכרין תקדיש קדם יי: יג וכל פתח בוכרא דחמרא תפרוק באימרא ואם לא תפרוק ותנקפיה וכל בוכרא דאנשא בבנך תפרוק: יד ויהי ארי ישאלנך ברך מחר למימר מא דא ותימר ליה בתקוף ידא אפקנא יי ממצרים מבית עבדותא: טו והוה כד אקשי פרעה לשלחותנא וקטל יי כל בוכרא בארעא דמצרים מבוכרא דאנשא ועד בוכרא דבעירא על כן אנא דבח קדם יי כל פתח ולדא דכריא וכל בוכרא דבני אפרוק: טז ויהי לאת על ידך ולתפילין בין עינך ארי בתקוף יד אפקנא יי ממצרים: ס ס ס

[illegible]

8

רמבן　　ספורנו

[illegible]

אבן עזרא   שמות יג בא   רשי

[illegible]

בדברי אגדה המושכין את הלב: (ח) בעבור זה. בעבור שאקיים מצותיו כגון פסח מצה ומרור הללו: עשה ה' לי. רמז תשובה לבן רשע לומר עשה ה' לי ולא לך שאלו היית שם לא היית כדאי ליגאל (מכילתא): (ט) והיה לך לאות. יציאת מצרים תהיה לך לאות על ידך ולזכרון בין עיניך רוצה לומר שתכתוב פרשיות הללו ותקשרם בראש ובזרוע: על ידך. יד שמאל לפיכך ידכה מלא בפרשה שניה לדרוש בה יד שהיא כהה (מכילתא מנחות לז): (י) מימים ימימה. משנה לשנה (שם לו) [illegible]

ז מצות יאכל את שבעת הימים ולא יראה לך חמץ ולא יראה לך שאר בכל גבלך: ח והגדת לבנך ביום ההוא לאמר בעבור זה עשה יהוה לי בצאתי ממצרים: ט והיה לך לאות על ידך ולזכרון בין עיניך למען תהיה תורת יהוה בפיך כי ביד חזקה הוצאך יהוה ממצרים: י ושמרת את החקה הזאת למועדה מימים ימימה: פ יא והיה כי יבאך יהוה אל ארץ הכנעני כאשר נשבע לך ולאבתיך ונתנה לך: יב והעברת כל פטר רחם ליהוה וכל פטר שגר בהמה אשר יהיה

ז פטירא יתאכיל ית שבעת יומין ולא יתחזי לך חמיע ולא יתחזי לך חמיר בכל תחומך: ח ותחוי לברך ביומא ההוא למימר בדיל דא עבד יי לי במפקי ממצרים: ט ויהי לך לאת על ידך ולדכרנא בין עינך בדיל דתהי אוריתא דיי בפומך ארי ביד תקיפא אפקך יי ממצרים: י ותטר ית קימא הדין בזמניה מזמן לזמן: יא ויהי ארי יעלינך יי לארע כנענאי כמא די קים לך ולאבהתך ויתנינה לך: יב ותעבר כל פתח ולדא קדם יי וכל פתח ולד בעירא דיהון לך

[illegible]

ספורנו

[illegible]

רמבן

[illegible]

1

2

3

4

5

6

7

5 RAMBAN, commentary by the Spanish rabbi Naḥmanides (1194-1270). The name **Ramban** derives from **Ra**bbi **M**oshe **b**en **N**aḥman.

6 SFORNO, by Obadiah ben Jacob, a sixteenth-century Italian rabbi. The commentary is named for the city where he lived.

7 OR HAḤAYYIM, by Ḥayyim ben Moses ibn Attar (1696-1743), a Moroccan rabbi whose work had great influence among the Ḥasidim.

8 BA'AL HATURIM, by Rabbi Jacob ben Rabbenu Asher (1270?-1340), author of the Tur (see Chapter 1, "Major Halakhic Authorities"). His commentary on Ḥumash includes many examples of **gematria**, explanations of words and phrases based on calculations of the numerical value of the Hebrew letters.

Because these five books contain the 613 commandments, you often hear the word "Torah" translated as "The Law." But this is only partially correct, since Ḥumash contains not only the 613 mitzvot but also the narratives of the patriarchs, the exodus, and the wilderness wanderings. Into these narratives and mitzvot the Torah weaves the major ideas, attitudes, and founding personalities of Jewish life. Their stories are our history, helping us develop our own life stories.

Since תּוֹרָה is directly related to the word for "teacher," **moreh** (מוֹרֶה), some people translate "Torah" as "The Teaching." But the truth is that none of these translations properly conveys the many layers of meaning that Jews have invested in the word "Torah." Through the ages, "Torah" has come to mean writings in every field of Jewish study, including ethics, justice, religion, and education.

TORAH SHEBIKHTAV AND TORAH SHEB'AL PEH

Because the Torah was passed down from generation to generation on a written scroll—meticulously guarded against even the slightest mistakes that might occur while copying and using it—it is called **Torah shebikhtav** (תּוֹרָה שֶׁבִּכְתָב), the "Written Torah." The term "Torah shebikhtav" can mean just the Ḥumash, but it may also refer to the entire Bible, which includes the Ḥumash; the Prophets, or **Nevi'im** (נְבִיאִים); and other general writings, known as **Ketuvim** (כְּתוּבִים). In Hebrew we call the entire Bible the **Tanakh** (תַּנַ"ךְ), an acronym based on the first letters of the Hebrew words תּוֹרָה, נְבִיאִים, and כְּתוּבִים.

At the same time the Jewish people received the Torah shebikhtav, they also received an oral explanation of the Torah through Moses. Without this oral explanation, we would be unable to understand the Torah in a Jewish way. The very first verse of Avot describes the origins of the Spoken Torah, or **Torah sheb'al peh** (תּוֹרָה שֶׁבְּעַל פֶּה):

Moses received the Torah on Sinai, and passed it on to Joshua; Joshua passed it to the elders; the elders passed it to the prophets; and the prophets passed it down to the Men of the Great Assembly (Avot 1:1).

At first these explanations and elaborations which comprised the Torah sheb'al peh were not allowed to be written down. They were conveyed from generation to generation just as Moses had taught them, **b'al peh** (בְּעַל פֶּה), "by word of mouth." They had to be studied, understood, repeated often, and then committed to memory.

SIFREI KODESH

Around 200 C.E., because of the fear that the Spoken Torah might be lost as Jews were dispersed around the globe, much of the Torah sheb'al peh was written down in the **Mishnah** (מִשְׁנָה). The word "Mishnah" comes from the Hebrew word **shanah** (שָׁנָה), which means

"The teaching of the Lord is perfect, renewing life" (Ps. 19:8).

"to repeat" or "to teach." This shows that the Mishnah was taught through repetition. "Shanah" is also related to the Hebrew word for "sharpen," and sounds like the Hebrew words for "year" and "change." This play on words gives us a picture of how the Mishnah gets transmitted to us—by study and repetition, by sharpening our minds, by helping us understand the changes around us as the years progress, and by showing us how Torah is able to relate to ever-changing situations.

The **Gemara** (גְּמָרָא)—the Aramaic root גמר means "learning"—contains explanations and traditions which the rabbis of later generations gathered to clarify the teachings of the Mishnah. Taken together, Mishnah and Gemara make up the **Talmud** (תַּלְמוּד); in comtemporary usage, however, the term "Gemara" sometimes refers to the entire Talmud. The rabbis of the Mishnah and Gemara use the word "Torah" to mean both the Torah shebikhtav and the Torah sheb'al peh.

Although we now have the Torah sheb'al peh, or Spoken Torah, in a written form, much about it still reminds us of its origins. The Talmud is arranged so that discussions, arguments, and counter-arguments from many generations stand side-by-side on the same page. And it is traditionally studied aloud and in pairs. Students of

Books of the Tanakh

FIVE BOOKS OF MOSES/ ḤUMASH (חוּמָשׁ)

ENGLISH TITLE	HEBREW TITLE
Genesis	בְּרֵאשִׁית
Exodus	שְׁמוֹת
Leviticus	וַיִּקְרָא
Numbers	בְּמִדְבַּר
Deuteronomy	דְּבָרִים

PROPHETS/ NEVI'IM (נְבִיאִים)

ENGLISH TITLE	HEBREW TITLE
Joshua	יְהוֹשֻׁעַ
Judges	שׁוֹפְטִים
I Samuel	שְׁמוּאֵל א
II Samuel	שְׁמוּאֵל ב
I Kings	מְלָכִים א
II Kings	מְלָכִים ב
Isaiah	יְשַׁעְיָה
Jeremiah	יִרְמְיָה
Ezekiel	יְחֶזְקֵאל
Hosea	הוֹשֵׁעַ
Joel	יוֹאֵל
Amos	עָמוֹס
Obadiah	עוֹבַדְיָה
Jonah	יוֹנָה
Micah	מִיכָה
Nahum	נַחוּם
Habakkuk	חֲבַקּוּק
Zephaniah	צְפַנְיָה
Haggai	חַגַּי
Zechariah	זְכַרְיָה
Malachi	מַלְאָכִי

WRITINGS/ KETUVIM (כְּתוּבִים)

ENGLISH TITLE	HEBREW TITLE
Psalms	תְּהִלִּים
Proverbs	מִשְׁלֵי
Job	אִיּוֹב
Song of Songs	שִׁיר הַשִּׁירִים
Ruth	רוּת
Lamentations	אֵיכָה
Ecclesiastes	קֹהֶלֶת
Esther	אֶסְתֵּר
Daniel	דָּנִיאֵל
Ezra	עֶזְרָא
Nehemiah	נְחֶמְיָה
I Chronicles	דִּבְרֵי הַיָּמִים א
II Chronicles	דִּבְרֵי הַיָּמִים ב

Talmud continue the venerated tradition of commenting, reading aloud enthusiastically, debating and discussing (while their hands gesture wildly), and passing new insights on to younger students by word of mouth.

The word "Torah" is sometimes used to mean all the sacred writings, or **sifrei kodesh** (סִפְרֵי קֹדֶשׁ), of the Jewish people. These include the entire Tanakh; the Talmud; the **Midrash** (מִדְרָשׁ), the collected moral teachings, sermons, and stories of the rabbis; and the codes of law, such as the Mishneh Torah and Shulḥan Arukh. Also included among the sifrei kodesh are the questions and problems sent by Jewish communities to the great Jewish scholars of the age,

Talmud should not be read but sung; not passively, but actively; not silently, but aloud; not alone, but in pairs.

together with the answers and solutions the scholars provided. These writings are called **responsa** or, in Hebrew, **she'elot u'teshuvot** (שְׁאֵלוֹת וּתְשׁוּבוֹת). As the sages said:

Turn [the Torah], and turn it again, for everything is in it; think of it, and grow old and grey as you study it, and never leave it, for you can have no better guide than this (Avot 5:22).

REWARDS FOR TORAH STUDY

In *Halakhic Man*, Rabbi Joseph Soloveitchik, a great American scholar and teacher, tells how Torah and the Jewish way of life are tied to one another:

When halakhic man approaches reality, he comes with his Torah, given to him from Sinai, in hand. He orients himself to the world by means of fixed statutes and firm principles. An entire corpus of precepts and laws guides him along the path leading to existence (p. 19).

Torah is thus an approach to life, a means by which we understand the world and our place in it. Yet Torah, in its broadest sense, is so vast that it seems impossible to know it all. How can one person ever grasp so great a treasure?

This is not a new problem. The rabbis of the Talmud knew that some people would look at the whole of the Torah and say, "It is too much to study, too much to learn." The rabbis recognized that some people might even give up in advance, refusing to study any Torah because they knew they could never know it all. To these people, Rabbi Tarfon said:

It is not your duty to complete the work, but you are not free to leave it undone; if you have studied much Torah, much reward will be given to you, for your Employer [HaShem] is faithful to pay you the salary for your work; and you should know that the promised reward for the righteous will be in the world to come (Avot 2:16).

Rabbi Tarfon says that those who study Torah will receive their reward in the world to come. As for rewards in this world, Jewish tradition holds that the best study of Torah is **Torah lishmah** (תּוֹרָה לִשְׁמָהּ), "Torah for its own sake." Even if you start with some other reason for studying Torah—for example, because you want to please your parents and teachers—if you study regularly, eventually your Torah study will become lishmah.

The true rewards for Torah study are summed up in a beautiful passage from the Mishnah:

These are the things to which no limit is set: [leaving] the corner of the field [for the needy], [the amount of] the first fruits [to bring to the Temple], the offering brought on the three pilgrimage festivals, the practice of kindness, and the study of Torah.

These are the things of which the fruits are enjoyed in this world while the capital remains for the world to come: honoring parents, kindness, bringing peace between people, and also the study of Torah, which is equal to them all (Pe'ah 1:1).

A DAILY RESPONSIBILITY

The Shulḥan Arukh addresses the primacy of studying Torah very plainly:

Everyone should set a certain time for the study of the Torah after praying, and this time should not be used for any other purpose. . . . If one has very important business to do, one should first study at least one verse of the Torah or one law, then attend to one's affairs and after that complete the regular assignment (Kitzur S.A. 27:1).

M'darf Lernen!

The story is told of a small band of Polish Jews trapped in occupied Eastern Europe at the end of the Holocaust period. Having avoided capture by the Nazis, they were now fleeing westward across Poland, hoping to escape the Soviet-controlled area to find freedom in the American zone.

After weeks of walking, the weary travelers arrived at the little town where they had all lived before the war. The town was reduced to rubble, and the synagogue had been destroyed. But an old stairway leading to a cellar had been preserved. There a few pious Jews found some volumes of Talmud, damaged by water but still readable. Immediately they lit candles and began to study in the traditional way—chanting, gesturing, davening.

From the top of the steps, one of their companions urged them to hurry.

"We're fleeing for our lives!" he cried. "The border may close any day now. The American zone is still far off. We've got to reach the border as soon as possible."

But one of the pious Jews waved the man away.

"Quiet," he said. "*M'darf lernen.* We must learn." And so the small group of Jews continued to study, before resuming their weary walk to freedom.

Source: Ludwig Lewisohn, What Is This Jewish Heritage? (New York: B'nai B'rith Hillel Foundations, 1957).

The Torah is an open book to all who wish to learn it.

Many of today's Jewish schools teach not only the ancient texts but also the skills and knowledge people need for earning a living in the modern world.

Some people have enough self-discipline to set aside a regular time for daily study. Many others are not "self-starters": they need more help. So Judaism does not leave the matter of when and what to study entirely up to the individual. The siddur includes the minimum daily study requirement for both Torah shebikhtav and Torah sheb'al peh: three verses of Ḥumash, three portions of Mishnah, and three of Gemara are a regular part of every tefillah. Even saying the Shema is a way of studying a portion of the Torah—and we do this daily, morning and night. The very first request of the middle thirteen blessings of the Shemoneh Esreh is a petition for understanding and wisdom. In addition, special portions of tefillah are devoted entirely to study.

Four times a week—on Monday, on Thursday, and twice on Shabbat—we include the reading of the Torah in our regular davening. Over the course of a year, from one Simḥat Torah to the next, we complete the reading of the entire Torah shebikhtav. This is another way in which Judaism sets a fixed time for study.

Although, strictly speaking, the mitzvah of Torah study requires you to study the Torah itself, Torah study in its widest sense is not confined to Torah shebikhtav and Torah sheb'al peh. Everything in life somehow ties in with Jewish learning, because Jewish learning has dealt with every aspect of human life, both good and bad. This is one reason the Jews have been called the "people of the book."

In the following passage from *Halakhic Man*, Rabbi Soloveitchik describes the relationship between the natural world and our duty to observe the commandments of Torah:

When halakhic man looks to the western horizon and sees the fading rays of the setting sun or to the eastern horizon and sees the first light of dawn and the glowing rays of the rising sun, he knows that this sunset or sunrise imposes upon him anew obligations and commandments. Dawn and sunrise obligate him to fulfill those commandments that are performed during the day: the recitation of the morning Shema, tzitzit, tefillin, the morning prayer, etrog, shofar, Hallel, and the like. . . . Sunset imposes upon him those obligations and commandments that are performed during the night: the recitation of the evening Shema, matzah, the counting of the omer, etc. . . . When he goes out on a clear, moonlit night . . . he makes a blessing upon it. He knows that it is the moon that determines the times of the months and thus of all the Jewish seasons and festivals, and this determination must rely upon astronomical calculations (pp. 20-21).

The world you create for yourself must begin with study, and all study must remind you of the study of Torah. The mitzvah "And you shall think on it by day and by night" refers specifically to the study of Torah shebikhtav and Torah sheb'al peh. It is over this study —which, for a Jew, is the foundation of all learning—that we recite three special berakhot each morning:

בָּרוּךְ אַתָּה, יהוה אֱלֹהֵינוּ, מֶלֶךְ הָעוֹלָם, אֲשֶׁר קִדְּשָׁנוּ בְּמִצְוֹתָיו וְצִוָּנוּ
לַעֲסוֹק בְּדִבְרֵי תוֹרָה.

Blessed are You, Lord, our God, King of the universe, who has sanctified us through His commandments and has commanded us to busy ourselves with words of Torah.

וְהַעֲרֶב־נָא, יהוה אֱלֹהֵינוּ, אֶת־דִּבְרֵי תוֹרָתְךָ בְּפִינוּ, וּבְפִי עַמְּךָ בֵּית
יִשְׂרָאֵל, וְנִהְיֶה אֲנַחְנוּ וְצֶאֱצָאֵינוּ, וְצֶאֱצָאֵי עַמְּךָ בֵּית יִשְׂרָאֵל, כֻּלָּנוּ
יוֹדְעֵי שְׁמֶךָ וְלוֹמְדֵי תוֹרָתֶךָ לִשְׁמָהּ. בָּרוּךְ אַתָּה, יהוה, הַמְלַמֵּד תּוֹרָה
לְעַמּוֹ יִשְׂרָאֵל.

Please, Lord, our God, sweeten the words of Your Torah in our mouth and in the mouth of Your people, the House of Israel. May we and our offspring, and the offspring of Your people, the House of Israel—all of us—know Your name and study Your Torah for its own sake. Blessed are You, Lord, who teaches Torah to His people Israel.

בָּרוּךְ אַתָּה, יהוה אֱלֹהֵינוּ, מֶלֶךְ הָעוֹלָם, אֲשֶׁר בָּחַר־בָּנוּ מִכָּל־הָעַמִּים
וְנָתַן־לָנוּ אֶת־תּוֹרָתוֹ. בָּרוּךְ אַתָּה, יהוה, נוֹתֵן הַתּוֹרָה.

Blessed are You, Lord, our God, king of the universe, who selected us from all the peoples and gave us His Torah. Blessed are You, Lord, giver of the Torah.

These blessings cover your Torah study for the whole day.

TORAH AND WORK

Which is more important: to work hard and earn a living for your family, or to spend your time studying Torah? That is the issue the following story raises.

עין משפט נר מצוה

מסורת הש"ס

מאימתי

מאימתי קורין את שמע בערבין. *משעה שהכהנים נכנסים לאכול בתרומתן עד סוף האשמורה הראשונה דברי ר' אליעזר. וחכמים אומרים עד חצות. רבן גמליאל אומר עד שיעלה עמוד השחר. מעשה ובאו בניו מבית המשתה אמרו לו לא קרינו את שמע אמר להם אם לא עלה עמוד השחר חייבין אתם לקרות ולא זו בלבד אמרו אלא *כל מה שאמרו חכמים עד חצות מצותן עד שיעלה עמוד השחר *הקטר חלבים ואברים מצותן עד שיעלה עמוד השחר *וכל הנאכלים ליום אחד מצותן עד שיעלה עמוד השחר א"כ למה אמרו חכמים עד חצות *כדי להרחיק אדם מן העבירה: גמ' *תנא היכא קאי דקתני מאימתי ותו מאי שנא (א) דתני בערבית ברישא לתני דשחרית ברישא תנא אקרא קאי *דכתיב בשכבך ובקומך והכי קתני זמן קריאת שמע דשכיבה אימת משעה שהכהנים נכנסין לאכול בתרומתן ואי בעית אימא יליף מברייתו של עולם דכתיב ויהי ערב ויהי בקר יום אחד אי הכי סיפא דקתני *בשחר מברך שתים לפניה ואחת לאחריה ובערב מברך שתים לפניה ושתים לאחריה לתני דערבית ברישא. תנא פתח בערבית והדר תני בשחרית עד דקאי בשחרית פריש מילי דשחרית והדר פריש מילי דערבית: אמר מר משעה שהכהנים נכנסים לאכול בתרומתן. מכדי כהנים אימת קא אכלי תרומה משעת צאת הכוכבים לתני משעת צאת הכוכבים. מלתא אגב אורחיה קמשמע לן כהנים אימת קא אכלי בתרומה משעת צאת הכוכבים והא קמשמע לן *דכפרה לא מעכבא כדתניא *ובא השמש וטהר ביאת שמשו מעכבתו מלאכול בתרומה ואין כפרתו מעכבתו מלאכול בתרומה. *וממאי דהאי ובא השמש ביאת השמש והאי וטהר טהר יומא דילמא

רש"י

מאימתי קורין את שמע בערבין. משעה שהכהנים נכנסים לאכול בתרומתן. כהנים שנטמאו וטבלו והעריב שמשן והגיע עתם לאכול בתרומה: עד סוף האשמורה הראשונה. שליש הלילה כדמפרש בגמ' (דף ג.) ומשם ואילך עבר זמן דלא מקרי תו זמן שכיבה ולא קרינן ביה בשכבך ומקמי הכי נמי לאו זמן שכיבה לפיכך הקורא קודם לכן לא יצא ידי חובתו. אם כן למה קורין אותה בבית הכנסת כדי לעמוד בתפלה מתוך דברי תורה והכי תניא בברכות ירושלמי. ולפיכך חובה עלינו לקרותה משתחשך. ובקריאת פרשה ראשונה שאדם קורא על מטתו יצא: עד שיעלה עמוד השחר. שכל הלילה קרוי זמן שכיבה: הקטר חלבים ואברים. של קרבנות שנזרק דמן ביום: מצותן. להעלות כל הלילה ואינן נפסלים בלינה עד שיעלה עמוד השחר והן למטה מן המזבח דכתי' לא ילין לבקר (שמות לד): חלבים. של כל קרבנות: אברים. של עולה: וכל הנאכלים ליום אחד. כגון חטאת ואשם וכבשי עצרת ומנחות ותודה: מצותן. זמן אכילתן: עד שיעלה עמוד השחר. והוא מביאן להיות נותר דכתיב בתודה לא יניח ממנו עד בקר (ויקרא ז) וכלם מתודה ילמדו: אם כן למה אמרו חכמים עד חצות. בקריאת שמע ובאכילת קדשים: כדי להרחיק אדם מן העבירה. ואסרום באכילה קודם זמנן כדי שלא יבא לאכלן לאחר עמוד השחר ויתחייב כרת. וכן בקריאת שמע לזרז את האדם שלא יאמר יש לי עוד שהות ובתוך כך יעלה עמוד השחר ועבר לו הזמן. והקטר חלבים דקתני הכא לא אמרו בו חכמים עד חצות כלל ולא נקט להו הכא אלא להודיע שכל דבר הנוהג בלילה כשר כל הלילה. והכי נמי תנן בפרק שני דמגילה (דף כ:) כל הלילה כשר לקצירת העומר ולהקטר חלבים ואברים: גמ' היכא קאי. מהיכא קא סליק דתנא ביה חובת קריאת שמע שהתחיל לשאול כאן זמן הקריאה: אקרא קאי. ושם למד חובת הקריאה: ואיבעית אימא. הא דתנא ערבין ברישא יליף מברייתו של עולם: והדר תנא בשחרית. מאימתי קורין את שמע בשחרית: משעת צאת הכוכבים. שהוא גמר ביאת השמש כדיליף לקמן (עמוד ב): דילמא

תוספות

מאימתי קורין וכו'. פי' רש"י ואנן היכי קרינן מבעוד יום ואין אנו ממתינין לצאת הכוכבים כדמפרש בגמ' על כן פירש רש"י שקריאת שמע שעל המטה עיקר והוא לאחר צאת הכוכבים. והכי איתא בירושלמי אם קרא קודם לכן לא יצא ואם כן למה אנו מתפללין קריאת שמע בבית הכנסת כדי לעמוד בתפלה מתוך דברי תורה. תימה לפירושו והלא אין העולם רגילין לקרות סמוך לשכיבה אלא פרשה ראשונה (לקמן דף ס:) ואם כן שלש פרשיות היה לו לקרות. ועוד קשה דצריך לברך בקריאת שמע שתים לפניה ושתים לאחריה בערבית. ועוד דאותה קריאת שמע סמוך למטה אינה אלא בשביל המזיקין כדאמר בסמוך (דף ה.) ואם תלמיד חכם הוא אינו צריך. ועוד קשה דא"כ פסקינן כרבי יהושע בן לוי דאמר תפלות באמצע תקנום פי' באמצע בין שני קריאת שמע בין קריאת שמע של שחרית ובין ק"ש של ערבית. ואנן קי"ל כר' יוחנן דאמר לקמן (דף ד:) איזהו בן העולם הבא זה הסומך גאולה של ערבית לתפלה. לכן פי' ר"ת דאדרבה קריאת שמע של בית הכנסת עיקר. ואם תאמר היאך אנו קורין כל כך מבעוד יום. ויש לומר דקיימא לן כרבי יהודה דאמר בפרק תפלת השחר (דף כו.) דזמן תפלת מנחה עד פלג המנחה דהיינו אחד עשר שעות פחות רביע ומיד כשיכלה זמן המנחה מתחיל זמן ערבית. ואם תאמר היאך אנו מתפללין תפלת מנחה סמוך לחשכה ואפילו לאחר פלג המנחה. יש לומר דקיימא לן כרבנן דאמרי זמן תפלת המנחה עד הערב ואמרינן לקמן (דף כז.) השתא דלא אתמר הלכתא לא כמר ולא כמר דעבד כמר עבד ודעבד כמר עבד. מכל מקום קשיא דהוי כתרי קולי דסתרן אהדדי שהרי מאיזה טעם אנו מתפללין ערבית מיד לאחר פלג המנחה משום דקיימא לן דשעת המנחה כלה כדברי רבי יהודה ומיד הוי זמן ערבית ובזמן התפלה עצמה לא קיימא לן כרבי יהודה אלא כרבנן. על כן אומר ר"י דודאי קריאת שמע של בית הכנסת עיקר ואנו שמתפללין ערבית מבעוד יום סבירא לן כהני תנאי דגמרא דאמרי משעה שקדש היום וגם משעה שבני אדם נכנסים להסב דהיינו סעודת ע"ש והיא היתה מבעוד יום ומאותה שעה הוי זמן תפלה. וגם ראיה (לקמן כז) דרב הוי מצלי של שבת בערב שבת ומסתמא גם היה קורא קריאת שמע. מכל אותן הראיות משמע דקריאת שמע של בית הכנסת היא עיקר. והא דקאמר בירושלמי למה היו קורין בבהכ"נ וכו' אומר ר"ת שהיו רגילין לקרות ק"ש קודם תפלתם כמו שאנו רגילין לומר אשרי תחלה ואותה ק"ש אינה אלא לעמוד בתפלה מתוך דברי תורה. ומכאן נראה מי שקורא ק"ש על מטתו שאין לברך וגם אינו צריך לקרות אלא פרשה ראשונה: ליתני דשחרית ברישא. כדאשכחן בתמיד דכתיב של בקר תחלה: אי הכי סיפא דקתני שחרית ברישא. אי אמרת בשלמא דסמיך אקרא דבשכבך א"כ אינו מקפיד קרא אלא אק"ש. אלא אי אמרת דסמיך אקרא דברייתו של עולם א"כ קפיד אכל מילי א"כ סיפא דקתני וכו': מברך שתים לפניה וכו'. (ירושלמי) ושבע ברכות הוי כנגד שבע ביום הללתיך (תהלים קיט) ולא קא חשיב יראו עינינו דההיא ברכה תקנו רבנן כדי להמתין לחבריהם בבית הכנסת. ודוקא בבית הכנסת שלהם שהיו עומדים בשדה והם מסוכנים מן המזיקים אבל בבתי כנסיות שלנו אין צריכין להמתין לחבריהם אלא בלילה: והא קמ"ל דכפרה לא מעכבא. וא"ת הא תנינא חדא זימנא במס' נגעים (פי"ד) ומייתי לה בהערל (דף עד:) העריב שמשו אוכל בתרומה וי"ל דרגילות של משניות לאשמועינן בקוצר אף למה שמפורש כבר: דילמא

רב נסים גאון

תורה אור

הגהות הב"ח (א) גמ' דתני ערבית ברישא:

גליון הש"ס

1
2
3
4
5
6
7
8

A Page of Talmud

1 MISHNAH, the first great codification of the Oral Law, or Torah sheb'al peh, compiled by Rabbi Judah HaNasi in Eretz Yisrael around the year 200 C.E. The rabbinic authorities quoted in the Mishnah are called **Tanna'im** (תַּנָּאִים).

2 GEMARA, written record of the discussions of Jewish law, along with philosophy and ethics, by the rabbinic authorities who lived between 200 and 500 C.E. These authorities are called **Amora'im** (אֲמוֹרָאִים).

3 RASHI, the great biblical commentator (see "A Page of Ḥumash"). His explanations of the Talmud are likewise indispensable.

4 TOSAFOT (תּוֹסָפוֹת), literally, "additions"; collections of comments, generally based on Rashi, by French and German rabbis between the twelfth and fourteenth centuries. Notable among the **tosafists** was Rashi's grandson, Rabbi Jacob ben Meir Tam (c. 1100-1171), who is known as Rabbenu Tam.

5 GILYON HASHAS, by Rabbi Akiva Eger (1761-1837), a German scholar of extraordinary learning and piety.

6 EIN MISHPAT, NER MITZVAH, by a 16th-century Italian scholar and printer, Rabbi Joshua Boaz ben Simon Baruch. His legal notes list where the halakhot of the Talmud may be found in the major early codes, including the Mishneh Torah and the Tur (see Chapter 1, "Major Halakhic Authorities").

7 MESORET HASHAS, cross-references that indicate other places in the Talmud where the same issue is discussed.

8 HAGAHOT HABAḤ, textual emendations by Rabbi Joel ben Samuel Sirkes (1561-1640), a Polish scholar who was the father-in-law of the Taz (see "A Page of Shulḥan Arukh" in Chapter 1).

The principle of *Torah im derekh eretz* means that we must combine Torah study with worldly culture.

A master sent his servant to market to buy flour and salt. He gave the servant a flat dish to carry the two items, but told him to make sure to keep the flour and salt separate.

When the servant reached the market, he presented the dish to a shopkeeper, who first filled it with flour and then started to measure the salt. Remembering his master's instructions not to mix the flour and salt together, the slow-witted servant turned the dish over and asked the shopkeeper now to fill the top side with salt. Meanwhile, the flour fell to the ground.

When the servant returned home with his dish full of salt, his master asked him where the flour was. "Oh, very simple," the servant said, "it's on the other side. I kept the flour and salt separate, just as you told me." With that, the servant turned the dish upside down. The salt fell to the ground, leaving him with nothing at all.

In this story, the flour represents work, and the income that work brings. The salt represents Torah, the learning that preserves the Jewish people. The moral of the story is compelling. Just as we need both flour and salt to make bread, so we need both work and study to lead a fully Jewish life; if you try to have one without the other, you may end up with neither. Perhaps an even more profound lesson is that you shouldn't throw out something good like Torah just to get a job, and you shouldn't entirely ignore your work, even to fill your plate with Torah.

Rabbi Eleazar ben Azariah said . . . , "Where there is no flour, there is no Torah; where there is no Torah, there is no flour" (Avot 3:18).

What did Rabbi Eleazar mean by linking Torah and flour so closely? Flour is whatever feeds your body. Torah is what feeds your soul. It is a terrible thing to go without food; your body starves, and death draws near. But it is also terrible to live without Torah; your soul starves, and your spirit shrivels. Just as bread nourishes the body, so Torah nourishes the soul. Together they enable you to lead a healthy and productive life.

Judaism encourages you to choose the kind of work that is best for you. But whatever you choose as your profession, study of Torah must be part of your daily routine. In the following passage from the Midrash, "wife" is used as a metaphor for Torah:

Rabbi Judah the Prince said (in the name of the Pious Men): Get yourself a trade along with Torah, for this is the meaning of "Live joyfully with the wife whom you love." Why did he call them "the Pious Men"? Because among them were Rabbi Yose and Rabbi Simeon, who divided their time thus: A third for the Torah, a third for prayer, and a third for work. Some say that they labored in the Torah all the winter and at their work all the summer (Eccl. R. 9:9).

Just as adults combine study with work, children mingle study with play.

TORAH AND DEREKH ERETZ

According to Jewish tradition, Torah holds the key not only to all Jewish learning but also to what the rabbis called **derekh eretz** (דֶּרֶךְ אֶרֶץ), or "proper behavior."

Actually, the term "derekh eretz" has many levels of meaning. In Hebrew, דֶּרֶךְ means "way" or "path," and אֶרֶץ means "land"; thus, the literal meaning of דֶּרֶךְ אֶרֶץ is "the way of the land," or how people conduct themselves in a certain place. Sometimes the term is translated as "courtesy" or "manners"—acting politely and not offending anyone. Derekh eretz also means your occupation, what you do in order to get on in your daily life. A famous nineteenth-century German rabbi, Samson Raphael Hirsch, taught the principle of **Torah im derekh eretz**. By this principle he meant that we must study both Judaism (Torah) and worldly culture (derekh eretz) in order to make our way in the world.

The rabbis of the Talmud believed that Torah and derekh eretz were closely linked. In the passage in which Rabbi Eleazar ben Azariah draws a connection between Torah and flour, he begins by saying:

Where there is no Torah, there is no derekh eretz; and where there is no derekh eretz, there is no Torah (Avot 3:18).

In this sense, derekh eretz means behaving responsibly toward others day by day.

People sometimes claim that it is possible to behave responsibly—to be a good person—without believing in Torah. They say, "Just being a good person is enough." The truth is that we all know some Jews who lead good lives even without studying Torah.

This Jewish camp in Michigan schedules Torah study sessions along with summer fun.

This may make them good people, but it does not make them good Jews—and Torah demands more of Jews than of other people. Our sages taught that society cannot continue for more than a few generations without the moral imperative of Torah. Ultimately, without Torah, people wind up being little better than wild animals. Animals may be basically "good," in the sense that they don't intentionally harm others for vengeance or sport. Yet when wild animals are hungry, they fight ferociously, clawing each other without mercy. Very few animals are naturally kind, naturally merciful, or naturally good.

When people are the final judge of their own actions, they are very much like animals in the wild. The way of the human world is to imitate the worst in the animal world, the sort of behavior we call "dog eat dog." Derekh eretz is a refinement of what it means to be human—the "ways of pleasantness" toward which Torah has directed us for thousands of years.

Rabbi Soloveitchik speaks of "halakhic man" as one who uses the laws of Torah as a guide to responsible everyday behavior. It is Torah which teaches you the commandment to love others as you love yourself. It is Torah which teaches you that all people are created in

HaShem's image. It is Torah which teaches you to consider the needs of others—to feed the poor, to protect the weak, to live with compassion and decency. In this, as in almost everything you do, Torah is your guide to what is proper in daily life. Unlike other standards of behavior, Torah does not change. It remains a permanent and stable authority, no matter which passing fads the world may worship or which direction the pendulum of fashion swings. This is why the rabbis said, "Where there is no Torah, there is no derekh eretz; and where there is no derekh eretz, there is no Torah."

STUDY AND ACTION

Of course, it is possible to study the laws of Torah without living by them, to know them but not follow them. As one of the sages of Talmud observed,

> A person who does good works and has studied much Torah is like a cup with a base [which stands solidly]. But one who does evil, even though he has studied much Torah, is like a cup without a base. As soon as it is filled, the cup turns over and whatever was in it spills. . . . A person who does good works and has studied much Torah is like a horse that has a harness. But one who does evil, even though he has studied much Torah, is like a horse that has no harness. As soon as a rider climbs on its back, it throws him off headlong (ARN 24).

If you are unwilling to follow the laws of Torah, then all your Torah study will be of no use. But if you study Torah and follow its laws and teachings, you take the important step of "doing what is right in God's sight" (Exod. 15:26). And this step should encompass everything that is done every day, including

> . . . what is right in business, or in buying and selling. So you may learn that the one who conducts business, and buys and sells, in truth and honesty, and who is pleasing to others, is regarded as if that person had fulfilled the whole Torah (Mekhilta, Vayetze, Beshallah).

This may be one reason the berakhah before studying does not simply say that HaShem commanded us to study Torah. Instead, it says that HaShem commanded us "to busy ourselves with words of Torah." Whatever your "busyness," you should do it in tune with Torah.

One of the positive mitzvot given in the Torah is based on a verse in Deuteronomy: "Now therefore you shall write this song for me . . . " (31:19). The rabbis explained that when Moses said "this song" he meant the entire Torah (Sanh. 21b). Thus, each person is commanded to write, or have written, once in his or her life, a scroll of the Torah! Not only that, but the writing of this scroll, or **sefer Torah** (סֵפֶר תּוֹרָה), must be done according to all the traditional rules. It must be written out by a sofer, by hand, on parchment. The ink must be prepared in the traditional way, and the letters must be formed in the precise manner that soferim use. After the sefer Torah is written, it may not be sold, except to earn money for one of three specific purposes: to get married, to study Torah, or to ransom captives.

This mitzvah has often been observed through the purchase of a sefer Torah. When Jews buy a sefer Torah to keep at home or to lend to the bet knesset, this encourages the writing of more sifrei Torah. The majority of Jews, however, cannot afford the expense of buying a sefer Torah. In our own day—when we do not study from the scroll itself—the lesson to be learned from the mitzvah of writing Torah is that Jews must buy Jewish books, maintain a Jewish home library, and do everything possible to keep Jewish learning alive.

KEEPING JEWISH LEARNING ALIVE

The obligation to keep Jewish learning alive is a mitzvah of its own. Morning and night you repeat the words of the Shema, "You shall teach them [the laws of Torah] diligently to your children . . . " (Deut. 6:7). It is your duty to pass on Jewish learning from one generation to the next. Women and men must learn, if only to teach those who follow. Your parents sent you to a school for Jewish learning because they want you to study your Jewish heritage. And you are asked to do the same for your children. By this commandment, every person is charged with the responsibility of being a teacher.

Although it is important to teach Torah to the young, it is equally important that all people study—no matter what their age or position

A sofer, or Torah scribe, must write out the sefer Torah by hand, on parchment, using the traditional tools and forming each letter in a prescribed way.

Hiddur mitzvah is the principle behind these beautifully decorated Torah ornaments. Right, the sefer Torah encased in the Sephardic manner; far right, a pair of ornately carved rimmonim; below, a silver Torah breastplate, made in Germany about 1750.

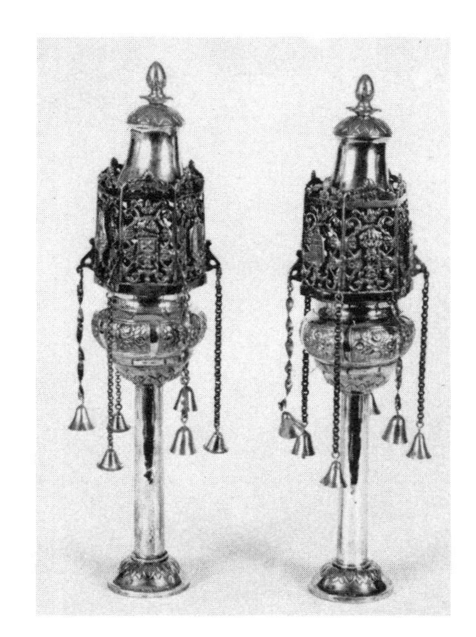

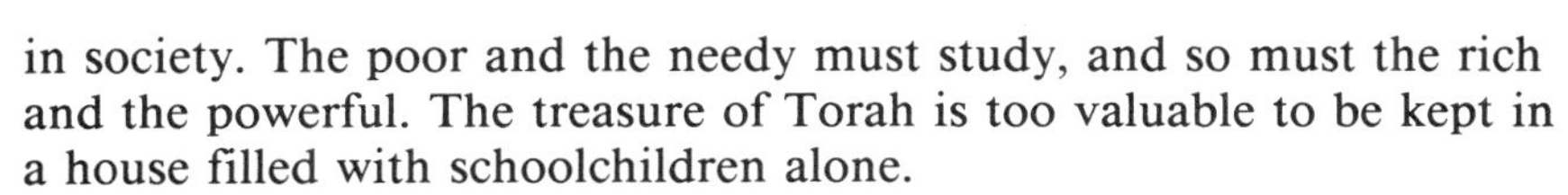

in society. The poor and the needy must study, and so must the rich and the powerful. The treasure of Torah is too valuable to be kept in a house filled with schoolchildren alone.

The rabbis of the Midrash recognized the unique value of Torah study:

> Can there be a transaction in which the giver gives not only the gift but his whole self as well? HaShem says, "I gave you My Torah, and with it, as it seems, I gave Myself." This is like a king who had but one daughter and another king asked to marry her and he did. The father said, "My daughter is an only child. I cannot be parted from her. Yet I cannot ask you to be parted from her, since she is your wife. Therefore, do me this favor: Wherever you go, make a place for me, that I may dwell with you." So HaShem says to Israel, "I have given you My Torah. I cannot be parted from it. Yet I cannot say to you, do not take it. Therefore, wherever you go, make Me a house, that I might dwell in it" (Ex. R. 33:1).

When you get something valuable, do you usually get its owner as well? Yet that is the way of Torah—for with it one also acquires, as it were, HaShem.

CHAPTER SEVEN

WORK

יָפֶה תַלְמוּד תּוֹרָה עִם דֶּרֶךְ אֶרֶץ.

An excellent thing is Torah combined with everyday work. . . .
(Avot 2:2)

Your life is made up of many parts. Part of each day is devoted to sleeping, part to eating, part to davening, part to studying Torah and other subjects, part to socializing and recreation. However, the major part of each work day is set aside for work.

When Jews think of work, our minds turn to the first work of all, the creation of the universe—HaShem's work.

The heaven and the earth were finished, and all that is in them. And on the seventh day God finished the work which He had been doing. And God ceased on the seventh day from all the work which He had done. And God blessed the seventh day and made it holy, because on it He ceased from all the work of creation which He had done (Gen. 2:1-3).

WORK AND SHABBAT

The Torah prizes human work not because it uses your muscles but because it exercises your brain. Work is meant to be a creative experience, and you should strive to do the kind of work that brings satisfaction. True satisfaction comes from using your imagination and ingenuity to accomplish something, not just from being paid for what you do.

One way to understand the meaning of work is to examine the kinds of work we are not permitted to do on Shabbat—the kinds of work important enough to be forbidden on the day of "rest." In the Talmud, an entire tractate discusses the categories of work that are prohibited. The Shulḥan Arukh applies these teachings, noting many intricate and important details. The basic idea in both places is the same. Work is any activity that is creative or that shows mastery of the world.

Baking, cooking, and making fire are examples of work. So are writing, drawing, and painting. It is work to prune trees, cut flowers, or weed the garden. Making things from wood and clay is work, as is

Whether you choose to be a bus driver or a college professor, Judaism encourages you to pursue the kind of worthwhile work that suits you best.

Categories of Work

The Talmud (Shab. 7:2) recognizes thirty-nine categories of work, called **melakhah** (מְלָאכָה). These categories represent a cross-section of the main types of human productivity.

Torah sheb'al peh teaches us that the melakhot prohibited on Shabbat are the ones used in building the desert Tabernacle, or **Mishkan** (מִשְׁכָּן). Constructing the Tabernacle required many different types of work, such as building and writing and plowing and shearing, all of which are creative and productive. The following list of the thirty-nine melakhot is adapted from *The Sabbath: A Guide to Its Understanding and Observance*, by Dayan Dr. I. Grunfeld:

1. Plowing
2. Sowing
3. Reaping
4. Sheaf making
5. Threshing
6. Winnowing
7. Selecting
8. Sifting
9. Grinding
10. Kneading
11. Baking
12. Sheep shearing
13. Bleaching
14. Combing raw materials
15. Dyeing
16. Spinning

17,18,19. Weaving activities

20. Separating into threads
21. Tying a knot
22. Untying a knot
23. Sewing
24. Tearing
25. Trapping or hunting
26. Slaughtering
27. Skinning
28. Tanning
29. Scraping pelts
30. Pattern making

any kind of construction. Sewing, knitting, and embroidery are work. So are hunting and fishing.

Studying Torah is not forbidden work. When we study, we are not trying to control the world, only to understand it better. So study is encouraged on Shabbat. Games are not work—in fact, you are permitted to play games and participate in other leisure activities that are reserved specifically for Shabbat and holidays. You can even play checkers, cards, chess, table tennis, or Scrabble. As long as you don't write down your scores or play for money, all of these are permitted.

The difference between what is permitted and what is prohibited on Shabbat has nothing to do with physical strain or exertion. For example, you're permitted to drag a heavy laundry bag from one room to another, but you're not permitted to carry a handkerchief outdoors. You could lift a table, but you may not flick on a light switch.

31. Cutting to shape
32. Writing
33. Erasing
34. Building
35. Demolishing
36. Kindling a fire
37. Extinguishing
38. The final hammer blow (putting the finishing touch on a newly made item)
39. Carrying from a private place to a public place (and vice versa)

Since these categories reflect Jewish agricultural practices and home life many hundreds of years ago, how do we relate them to the way we live today? Over the centuries, rabbis have applied the melakhot to the activities of their own time. Consider the following examples.

Writing: This category includes any sign or mark made in a durable manner. From the prohibition against writing on Shabbat we learn that we should not draw, paint, or embroider. We also learn that we may not use a computer, since when we save what is on the screen we make it durable (in addition to the fact that we use electricity to turn it on).

Building: This category includes constructing or repairing any object, or permanently joining or glueing two things to make an object. From the prohibition against building on Shabbat we learn that we should not knock a nail into the wall, put up a tent (or even open an umbrella), join a broom handle and a brush, or model clay.

Kindling a fire: This category includes anything that starts a fire or prolongs one. From the prohibition against kindling a fire on Shabbat we learn that we may not regulate a flame in the oven by turning it up or down, switch on a light, smoke a pipe or cigarette, or drive a car.

Most authorities say you can play Scrabble and other indoor games on Shabbat—as long as you don't write down your scores or play for money.

In their native lands the ḥalutzim may have been teachers, lawyers, or physicians, but in Eretz Yisrael they became farmers and builders.

In sum, when we speak of work, we mean things we do in order to be creative, just as HaShem was creative—and on the seventh day we rest, just as HaShem rested. HaShem encourages us to work six days a week so we can make the world a better place. In fact, without the work we perform throughout the week, Shabbat would not have the rich meaning it does. On this day, HaShem rested from all the work that He created as Master of the world. Thus, on Shabbat, people should also rest from being creative and trying to control the world.

WORK AS A DUTY

The sages did not just talk about the value of doing creative work. They also practiced what they preached. A few of the rabbis came from wealthy families and spent all their time in study, but most worked hard to earn their living. Rabbi Akiba collected and sold a bundle of firewood each day. Rabbi Judah was a baker; Abba Saul was first a gravedigger and later a kneader of dough. Rabbi Joshua was a charcoal burner. Rabbi Meir was a scribe. Rabbi Yosi ben Ḥalafta was a leather worker, and Rabbi Yoḥanan was a maker of sandals (ARN 6; J. Ḥag. 77b; Nid. 24b; Pes. 34a; Ber. 28a; Eruv. 13a; Shab. 49b; Avot 4:14). So the sages of the Talmud taught the importance of work by working.

The rabbis recognized that our world could hardly exist if all its inhabitants spent their whole time studying. For the world to survive—and for us to survive as complete human beings—we need both study and work. So the rabbis wrote:

An excellent thing is Torah combined with everyday work [derekh eretz], for the labor demanded by them both causes sin to be forgotten. All study of Torah without work must in the end be useless and become the cause of sin (Avot 2:2).

What sin could possibly come from the study of Torah? The rabbis understood that people who only studied Torah but did not work might begin to think they were more important than people who studied Torah part-time and also had to work for a living. They might become proud, forgetting that Torah teaches us to be humble. For this reason, even the study of Torah could lead to sin.

Rambam warns that if a person does not earn a livelihood, he will come to covet other people's possessions. Rambam himself was a physician, and many other great Jewish teachers and scholars worked at everyday tasks. The poet and philosopher Judah HaLevi was also a physician, and Rashi was a wine maker.

Our sages taught that we should divide our time in a way that allows for both study and work. Probably they overstated the case when they said:

If a person learns two paragraphs of Torah in the morning and two paragraphs in the evening, and is busy in work all the day, that person has fulfilled the Torah entirely (Tanḥ., Beshalah 20).

These Jews also work the land, growing cotton, wheat, and pecans in the Mississippi delta.

By this the rabbis did not really mean that four paragraphs of Torah study is enough. What they meant was that everyone should follow at least a minimum regular schedule of Torah study. If you do follow such a regular schedule, then you cannot be faulted if your work leaves you little additional time to study Torah.

In emphasizing the importance of work, our sages fancifully imagined that, even in the Garden of Eden, Adam was not able to eat until he had worked. How do we know this? The Torah says, "The Lord God took the man and put him into the Garden of Eden to work it and keep it" (Gen. 2:15). Only after this is it written, "Of every tree of the garden you may eat" (Gen. 2:16). In the same way, the people of Israel were told that they would have to work before the **Shekhinah** (שְׁכִינָה), God's presence, would dwell among them, as the Torah says, "Let them make for Me a sanctuary that I may dwell among them" (Ex. 25:8). The work of the Israelites was building the sanctuary.

To the rabbis, life and work were inextricably linked. The phrase "Therefore choose life" was interpreted by the rabbis to mean "choose a profession" (J. Pe'ah 15c). The degree to which the rabbis valued work can be seen in the following statement:

Rabbi Eliezer says: Even if [his wife had] a hundred servants [to do all the rest of her work] he should still ask her to work in wool, for idleness leads to sin (Ket. 5:5)

For women as well as men, work holds an honorable place in Jewish tradition. As long ago as the thirteenth and fourteenth centuries, pious Jewish women were serving as bankers, as agents of major businesses, and as financial trustees for Jewish communities. Their hard work soon made them economically independent, and many women made generous contributions to Jewish schools and toward the publication of books on halakhah.

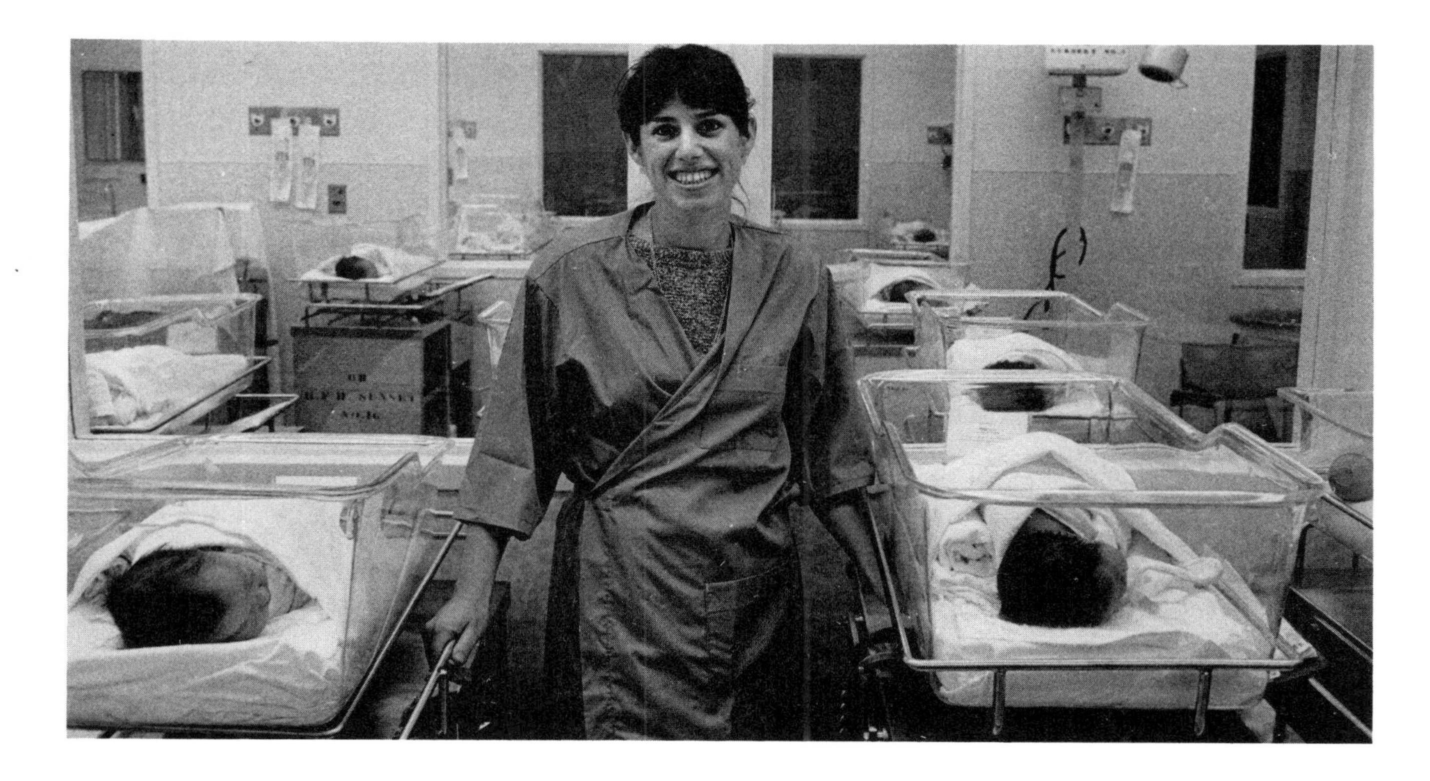

Work for these women means assisting in the miracle of life. Above, a Los Angeles pediatrician; opposite page, a poultry farmer on a kibbutz.

LIVING BY TORAH

During the second century C.E., Rabbi Simeon bar Yoḥai spoke out against the Roman order that no Torah should be studied in Eretz Yisrael. He and his son were forced to flee to a cave where, the Talmud tells us, they remained hidden for twelve years. During these years, they did nothing but sleep and eat and study Torah. By the twelfth year they seemed to glow with the fire of Torah learning.

At the end of the twelfth year, Rabbi Simeon and his son learned that the Roman emperor had died and the decree against Torah study had been lifted. At last, it was safe for them to come out of the cave.

They were approaching Jerusalem when Rabbi Simeon saw Jewish farmers tending their fields. All at once he was filled with rage. He called out to them angrily, saying, "How dare you waste your time this way? The decree of the Romans is lifted. We can study Torah again! Leave your fields and study!"

The farmers replied, "It is harvest time. We will study later."

Then Rabbi Simeon shouted to heaven, "Let these fields burn, for the people are doing work when they should be studying Torah." Wherever the rabbi and his son turned their eyes, the fields burst into flame.

Finally a voice came out of heaven, saying, "Have you left your cave to destroy My world? It is more important to live by Torah than to study it. Now go back to your cave and study your ways!"

And Rabbi Simeon and his son returned to their cave to study for another twelve months (Shab. 33b).

By this parable, the Talmud shows that Torah should not separate you from the everyday life of your community. Indeed, Torah helps you learn what it means to live a fully Jewish life even as you work. Through studying Torah, you learn how business people should deal with one another, how bargaining can be conducted fairly, and what obligations you have as someone else's boss or worker. There is a Jewish way of doing business which is detailed in Jewish law, and which can only be learned through the study of Torah.

WORK AND THE COMMUNITY

Whether your work involves physical labor or thinking labor, you can be certain of one thing: our community needs all the honest work it can get. We need physicians, lawyers, professors, and social workers, but we also need plumbers, roofers, farmers, and service technicians.

The Midrash tells of the time when Rabbi Yoḥanan passed a man digging a well. The man looked up and said, "Rabbi, did you know that I am as important as you?"

"Why is that?" Rabbi Yoḥanan asked.

"Because my work is as important to our community as yours is. You tell someone to go to the mikveh to take a ritual bath. But I'm the one who provides the water for them!" (Eccl. R. 4:17).

Each one of us depends on hundreds of other people every day of our lives. As it is written:

> Ben Zoma once saw a gathering of people on the Temple Mount. He said, "Blessed is HaShem, . . . who has created all these people to serve me."
>
> He explained: "What a great amount of work Adam had to do before he had bread to eat! He had to plow, to sow, to reap, to bind the sheaves, to thresh and to winnow. Then he had to select the ears, to grind them, to sift the flour, to knead, and to bake. At last he could eat bread. Whereas, I get up each morning and find all these things done for me!
>
> "And how many labors Adam had to carry out before he had clothing to wear! He had to shear, to wash the wool, to comb it, to spin it, and to weave it. At last he had clothing. Whereas, I get up and find all these things done for me!" (Ber. 58a).

CHOOSING A JOB

At this point you might be wondering: If all kinds of honest work are worthwhile, why do my parents want me to become a lawyer or doctor? Parents may want their children to enter law, medicine, or another profession for a variety of reasons, including how much money they can earn, how much of a contribution they can make to humanity, and how much mental stimulation the work provides. But whatever ambitions your parents may have for you, there is no great religious value in laboring at something you don't like or aren't fit for. We should make a lifelong avocation of helping others, even if our vocations are primarily designed to help ourselves.

Our history and tradition teach us that no honest work is too lowly. In our own time, we have the lesson of the pioneers, or

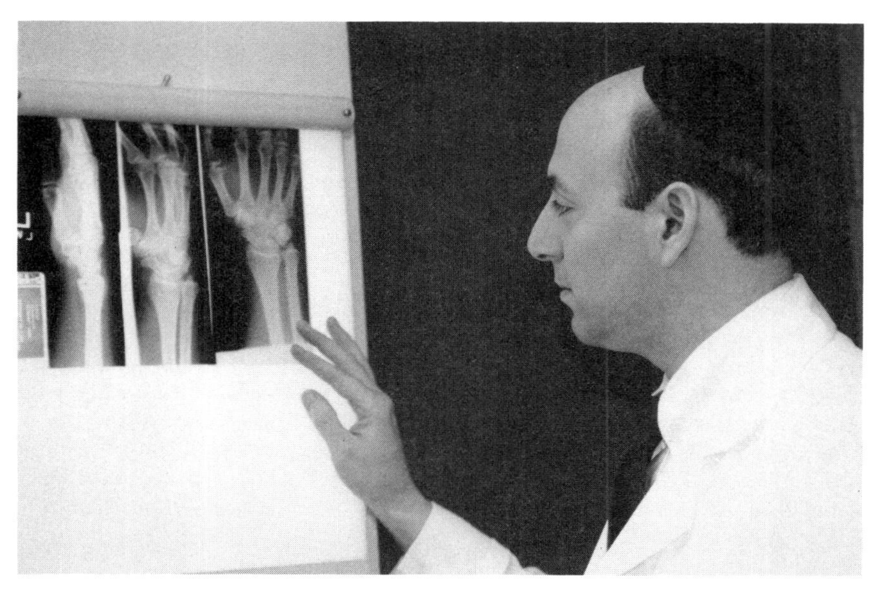

"Six days you shall labor" (Ex. 20:9). Satisfying this commandment also enables you to fulfill the mitzvah of tikkun olam—literally, improvement of the world. Two ways to improve the world are fixing broken pipes and mending broken bones.

ḥalutzim (חֲלוּצִים), who returned to Eretz Yisrael. They may have been teachers, lawyers, and physicians in the lands they came from, but in Israel they were satisfied to return to farming and building. They thought of this as proper work—and it is.

Naturally, some kinds of work are thought of as more important—after all, some people are paid very highly for their work, and others receive little pay for theirs. However, the Talmud teaches us that we must guard against the sin of false pride. All honest work is important if society is to remain healthy and productive. Whatever

Tikkun olam means repairing the world and making it a better place. "Do not call them your children [*banaikh*] but rather your builders [*bonaikh*]" (Shab. 114a).

work you choose is essential. In ancient times, people thought that being a shepherd was among the lowliest of professions. Yet Moses was a shepherd, and the Midrash says that it was Moses' concern for the stray sheep that made him a fit leader for the Jewish people.

Rabbi Ḥiyya ben Ami further said in the name of Ulla: A person who lives from the labor [of the hands] is greater than the person who fears heaven [but relies on support from other people]. For with regard to the one who fears heaven, it is written: "Happy is the one who fears God" (Ps. 112:1); while with regard to the one who lives by working, it is written: "When you eat the labor of your own hands, you shall be happy, and it shall be well with you" (Ps. 128:2). "You shall be happy" in this world, "and it shall be well with you" in the world to come. But of the one that fears heaven, it is not written: "and it shall be well with you" (Ber. 8a).

HONEST AND DISHONEST WORK

In Chapter 6 you read about a special way of looking at the world, the halakhic view described by Rabbi Joseph Soloveitchik. When we take the view of "halakhic man," all work could become kadosh. That is what Ben Zoma was saying as he looked out on the crowd on the Temple Mount. That is what the well digger was telling Rabbi Yoḥanan.

The rabbis taught, "A person is commanded to teach his child a trade, and whoever does not teach his child a trade, it is as if he teaches him to become a robber instead" (Kid. 30b). Are there any honest trades we are not permitted to teach our children?

"He has made everything beautiful in its time" (Eccl. 3:11). What does this verse mean? It teaches that the Holy One, the Blessed, makes every occupation agreeable in the eyes of those who practice it (Ber. 43b).

In the eyes of the halakhic Jew, all honest work is holy work. As the Talmud says, "Great is work for it honors the worker" (Ned. 49b). Earning our daily bread—making a living—gives meaning to our lives and adds to our personal kedushah. It carries not only the reward of a salary but also an inner reward of satisfaction.

Of course, some occupations are definitely not permissible—for example, selling illegal drugs, dealing in pornography, or buying and selling through the use of fraud, bribery, or coercion. Ambition for money or power makes some people work in ways which are outside the law. Even if the work they do is normally permitted, the way they do it may make it un-Jewish and improper. This is another lesson the Torah teaches. You must do your utmost to find work which is honest and honorable.

Honest labor brings you honest rewards. It brings justice to society, injecting a sense of honor into the workaday world. Your work gives you a chance to practice the mitzvot in a very direct and important way. It makes you a useful member of the community. It gives you the opportunity to make the world a better place in which to live.

Jewish law is concerned with the ethics of work—"giving an honest day's work" to your client or employer. For example, if you work for someone all day long, your employer must give you regular times to eat. But you must not stop again to eat during your workday.

As the owner is warned not to rob the poor of their wages and not to delay payment, so the worker is warned not to rob the employer by wasting time, a little here and a little there, and not giving a full day's service. . . . So, too, the worker must work with all his powers, as Jacob, our righteous father said (Gen. 31:6), "for with all my power I worked for your father." Therefore, he received his reward in this world, too, as it is said (Gen. 30:43), "and [Jacob] prospered very, very greatly" (M.T., Hilkhot Seḥirut, 13).

Jacob was successful, Rambam says, because he was honest in his work, gave it his full attention, and did it as well as he could.

CHEATING: THREE CASE STUDIES

At this moment, your work may be school. If you were in business—for example, if you were a butcher—you would have to follow many laws which call for honesty. You would have to be sure that your scales were exact, so that you did not cheat people when they bought meat by the pound. You would have to trim the meat carefully, so that people who bought from you would not be forced to buy too much fat. Of course, you are not a butcher, but laws like these are still important to you. The idea of an honest scale is a basic principle for all of life.

Honesty and integrity are as important in schoolwork as in any other occupation.

Cheating sometimes happens at school, just as it sometimes does in business. Consider these three cases.

Case One: Reuben and Simon sit next to each other in class. Reuben prepares carefully for an exam. He reviews everything the class has studied since the last test. Simon is not a good student. He tries to prepare, but never does well on tests. Simon comes to school on the day of the exam and tells Reuben that "everyone is going to be cheating today." During the exam, Simon leans over several times and copies from Reuben's paper. When the test papers are graded, each student gets an *A*. The teacher does not know that Simon cheated on the test.

Case Two: Rachel and Sarah are students in the same class. They are best friends. They often study together at home. One day, the teacher assigns a research paper. That afternoon, Rachel says to Sarah, "Let's do the work together. We can write one paper and then make a few changes, so the teacher thinks the papers are different."

Case Three: Benjamin is assigned to write a paper about the kibbutz in Israel. He goes to the school library during study time. In looking over the Israel shelf, he discovers a dust-covered book that is entirely about the kibbutz. Looking inside the cover, he finds that the book has not been signed out for the last eight years! Benjamin decides to take a chance. He copies his whole report, sentence by sentence, from the book. When the papers are returned, Benjamin is pleased because he received an *A*. At the top, the teacher writes, "Very, very well done!"

In evaluating these cases, it's tempting to think that what happens in school doesn't really matter very much; after all, school is not the creative work you will be doing for the rest of your life. But the rabbis did not underestimate the importance of schooling. Rabbi Judah the Prince said, "Do not keep children away from school even to help in building the Temple." And Resh Lakish said, "The world stands only upon the breath of students" (Shab. 119b). The importance of education is emphasized in many places throughout the Talmud. Because schooling is so important, the problem of cheating in school must be taken very seriously.

All three cases are examples of cheating. In Case One, Simon wants to do well on the test, and even prepares for it. But Simon is afraid of getting a low grade. Read the following comment by Rambam and then consider how it relates to Simon's problem:

> **A student must not feel ashamed on account of his classmates who have understood a subject almost immediately, while it takes him many times to grasp it. If he were to feel embarrassment because of this, he would be attending school without learning anything (M.T., Sefer Hamada, Hilkhot Talmud Torah, 4:5).**

Simon is not learning anything by copying from his classmate. Moreover, he is a thief. He is not stealing money, of course, but he is

"Great is work for it honors the worker" (Ned. 49b).

stealing another person's work, another person's knowledge. Simon is also guilty of **genevat da'at** (גְּנֵיבַת דַּעַת), or "mental deception," in trying to fool his teacher into believing that the answers on the test were his own.

The students in Case Two are also cheating. They are cheating themselves by not doing their own work. People can learn only through the work they do themselves. But the students are also cheating in another way; they are stealing their teacher's confidence. Furthermore, they are conspiring against their teacher, hoping to make the instructor look foolish. This is a serious offense, for halakhah contains cases in which our teachers are considered more important than our parents:

> **[If a person went to seek] his own lost property and that of his father, his own has first place; if his own and that of his teacher, his own has first place; if that of his father and that of his teacher, his teacher's has first place—for his father did but bring him into this world, but his teacher that taught him wisdom brings him into the World to Come.... If his father and his teacher were each taken captive, he must first ransom his teacher and afterward ransom his father... (B.M. 2:11).**

Conspiring to make a teacher look foolish is like trying to make a parent look foolish. And that is a very serious offense! Our teachers are very much like our parents, in more ways than one. The word for "teachers" in Hebrew is **morim** (מוֹרִים). The word for "parents" is **horim** (הוֹרִים). Both these words come from the same Hebrew root, which is also the root for תּוֹרָה. This root has two meanings, "to teach" and "to shoot" (as in aiming and shooting an arrow). Our teachers and our parents try to instruct us, and they also try to "aim" us in the right direction—in the direction that allows us to lead the healthiest, most productive, and most worthwhile lives.

In Case Three, Benjamin is alone, but he is still cheating. He is copying the work of another person. This kind of cheating is called **plagiarism**. To plagiarize is to steal someone else's ideas or writings and pretend that they are your own. This is cheating and theft at the same time, another kind of genevat da'at. Plagiarism is as wrong as if you put your hand into someone else's pocket and stole a dollar bill.

TAKING PRIDE IN WORK

Work should not only be done honestly; it should also be done well. You often hear people speak of "the pride of the workman." When you see, hear, feel, touch, or smell something which has been carefully crafted or artistically completed—whether it is a banister on a stairway or a painting by a great master, whether it is a fine perfume or a good book—you know that you have encountered something special and wonderful. There is character in it, along with honor and even piety. The person who created it gave it the fullest attention. It was not created just for the sake of a salary. It was created out of devotion.

Sometimes people rush through their work. They don't take care to finish it completely or well. But things done too quickly usually look that way. Jobs done with proper care have an inner beauty. Whatever the work you choose to do in life, the important thing to remember is that you must do it as if it were precious, unique in all the world.

The Ḥasidim tell a story about a rebbe who took his students to the circus. There they saw a man walking a tightrope.

One of the students asked, "Why is that man risking his life in this way?"

The rebbe answered, "I do not know why he has chosen this profession. But I do know this: as long as that man is walking that tightrope, he is using his whole mind and soul to concentrate on walking it. If, for one moment, he stopped to worry about the money that he is earning by walking the tightrope, he would lose his balance and fall to his death. Only while he concentrates on the work he is doing can he hope to succeed."

CHAPTER EIGHT

ḤESED

עולם חסד יבנה.

The world is built by ḥesed.

(Mekhilta, Shirah, Beshalah, ch. 9)

In a time much shorter than you may imagine, you will be choosing a career. If you are fortunate, you will find an occupation that not only enables you to earn a living but also helps make the world better.

Nevertheless, the world is a tough place. Things do not always go as planned. Nearly all people hope for success in the work they choose, but some will never achieve it. They may end up poor, though they hoped to be comfortable; they may end up hungry, though they wanted to help feed others; they may be average, though they expected to excel. There is no guaranteed way of knowing whether you will be completely successful or not.

Whether or not you are successful in the career you choose, there is another kind of activity you are urged to do. In Hebrew, we call it **ḥesed** (חֶסֶד); in English, this mitzvah is sometimes called "deeds of loving-kindness," or simply "kindness." As the Shulḥan Arukh says:

> A person should be mindful that just as he entreats HaShem every hour for his livelihood and prays that HaShem should hear his pleading, so should he hear the needs of the disadvantaged. Also he should be mindful that poverty is a wheel that turns in the world, and the end of man is that he or his child or grandchild will come to this very same circumstance—and he who has compassion for others will himself receive compassion (S.A., Yoreh De'ah, 247:3).

The subject of ḥesed is very complex. The word חֶסֶד is associated with **ḥasid** (חָסִיד), a pious person, though not necessarily one from a Ḥasidic grouping. The link between ḥesed and ḥasid shows us that kindness is not just admirable behavior but also a religious value, a form of piety that needs to become part of everything you do. Interestingly, on rare occasions, חֶסֶד can also mean "to shame" or "to revile." This connection may well arise from the fact that acts of kindness, when performed in a thoughtless or tactless manner, can bring shame on the person we are trying to help. Our tradition

In one yeshiva's "Big Brother" program, an older boy helps a younger student learn the alef-bet.

A kind word, a loving smile—ḥesed is an opportunity to go just a little beyond what is absolutely required.

requires us to go beyond the letter of the law, to look deep into the mitzvot to find the true spirit of the commandments. And that is how ḥesed needs to be offered. Like many other important activities, ḥesed grows in value as we grow in wisdom.

An important Jewish value closely connected with ḥesed is **raḥamim**, which means "compassion" or "mercy." In Hebrew, רַחֲמִים comes from **reḥem** (רֶחֶם), or "womb." Raḥamim suggests tenderness, warmth, love—a feeling of empathy for all of HaShem's creation. In showing raḥamim to all creatures, we imitate HaShem, who is often called HaRaḥamim, "the Compassionate."

TZEDAKAH

One kind of ḥesed is **tzedakah**, a mitzvah you already know something about. The Hebrew word צְדָקָה, which literally means "righteousness," comes from **tzedek** (צֶדֶק), meaning "justice" or "fairness."

"Tzedakah" is sometimes translated into English as "charity." Now "charity" comes from the Latin word *caritas*, which implies "giving"—out of the goodness of one's heart, and by someone of superior to someone of inferior social status. If you think of tzedakah as charity, you may get the impression that tzedakah is something you do only out of the kindness of your heart, to help someone who is less well off than you are. But that is only partly true.

In the Jewish world view, the essence of tzedakah flows from a grand idea, revolutionary in its nature, which pierced through the darkness of the primitive world:

> You shall love your neighbor as yourself: I am the Lord (Lev. 19:18).

Of course, "neighbor" does not mean only the person who lives next door. We are instructed also to love the stranger,

> . . . for you were strangers in the land of Egypt: I the Lord am your God (Lev. 19:34).

Thus, tzedakah is not merely an act of generosity, to be performed on impulse toward a social inferior. Tzedakah is a mitzvah, to be performed out of a sense of obligation to HaShem and love for our fellow human beings. Both the giver and receiver of tzedakah were created by HaShem. The tzedakah you give is your chance to set right the scales of tzedek—scales which are often upset by the injustices of the everyday world.

GIVING TO THE POOR

The mitzvah of giving to the poor is founded in biblical society. Farmers were instructed as to what they could reap and what should be set aside for strangers and the needy.

Before each Yom Tov, students at this Jewish day school show ḥesed to the Jewish poor and shut-ins by packing boxes of gefilte fish, ḥallah, and other traditional foods donated by Federation. "You give . . . open-handedly, feeding every creature to its heart's content" (Ps. 145:16).

When you reap the harvest of your land, you shall not reap all the way to the corners of your field, or gather the gleanings of your harvest. You shall not pick your vineyard bare, or gather the fallen fruit of your vineyard. You shall leave them for the poor and the stranger: I, the Lord, am your God (Lev. 19:9-10).

Three forms of tzedakah were given at the time of harvest, when the community took in its produce. They are described in the Torah and formulated into law in tractate Pe'ah of the Talmud. The first form of tzedakah is **leket** (לֶקֶט), which means the grain that falls in the process of harvesting the fields. The second is **shikh'ḥah** (שִׁכְחָה), the sheaves of grain that are forgotten and left behind in the process of harvesting; even what is left behind accidentally is to be considered tzedakah because of the good it does for the poor, who have no fields of their own to harvest. The third form of tzedakah is **pe'ah** (פֵּאָה), or the corners of the field, which must also be left for the poor.

The practice of shikh'ḥah is particularly interesting. A great sage made a party one day in honor of having forgotten to reap part of his field and thereby being enabled to perform this mitzvah. But why didn't he make a party for observing other mitzvot, such as pe'ah? The answer is that shikh'ḥah is the only mitzvah you can never perform consciously. You cannot intentionally forget—but if you do forget, you should give the forgotten portion to the poor. The sage thus made a party to show his gratitude for the memory lapse that enabled him to perform this rare mitzvah—a mitzvah he couldn't perform if he tried!

The Mishnah goes into great detail concerning the mitzvot of leket, shikh'ḥah, and pe'ah. Some of the practical laws include:

> The "corner" [pe'ah] should not be less than one-sixtieth part [of the harvest] (Pe'ah 1:2).
>
> If [two] brothers [who owned one parcel of land] separate [the land into two fields], they must leave two sets of "corners"; but if they again join the fields into one, they need only grant one set of "corners" (Pe'ah 3:5).
>
> What counts as "gleanings" [leket]? Whatever drops down at the moment of reaping. If a reaper reaped an armful or plucked a handful and a thorn pricked him and [what he reaped] fell to the ground, this still belongs to the owner of the field . . . (Pe'ah 4:10).
>
> If a person will not allow the poor to glean, or allows one and not another, or aids one of the poor, he is a robber of the poor . . . (Pe'ah 5:6).

Obviously, the laws of tzedakah deal with more than farmers and fields: they only start there. In the Shulḥan Arukh we see how they apply wherever Jews live. For example:

> It is a positive mitzvah to give tzedakah to the poor of Israel, as it is said (Deut. 15:8), "You shall surely open your hand . . . ," and it is said (Lev. 25:36), ". . . that your brother may live with you." Anyone who sees a poor man begging and turns his glance away from him and does not give him tzedakah sins against a negative command, as it is said (Deut. 15:7), "You shall not harden your heart nor shut your hand from your needy brother. . . . " A person should also take to heart that poverty is like a revolving wheel, and in the end he or his son or his son's son may be reduced to taking tzedakah. He should not think, therefore, "Why should I take from what is mine to give to the poor?" Instead, he should understand that what he has is not his, but only on loan to him in trust to do what the Depositor [HaShem] wishes . . . (S.A., Yoreh De'ah, 247:3, Rema).

Not only the rich must give tzedakah. The commandment applies to everyone in the community:

> Every person is commanded to give tzedakah according to his means, even a poor man who is supported by tzedakah. . . . Even if he can give only a small thing, he should not hold back, for his little is considered the same as much from a rich man. . . . However, if he has only enough for his bare survival, he is not asked to give tzedakah, for one's own support comes before anyone else's (S.A., Yoreh De'ah, 248:1-4).

This passage raises the question of how much tzedakah you should give. How do you determine how much you can afford? The tradition required Jews to **tithe**—that is, to give ten percent of their income to the poor. People were discouraged from impoverishing themselves by giving too much tzedakah. In the United States, where charitable contributions are tax deductible, people sometimes make the mistake of measuring how much they give by how much of a tax break they need, rather than by what is morally right. Nevertheless, Jews in the United States have been, on the whole, remarkably generous in their contributions to both Jewish and non-Jewish causes.

Direct grants of money or food are not the only ways to give tzedakah. Our sages recognized that among the best ways to assist a poor person are to help him learn a trade or to provide a loan so he can start his own business (Kitzur S.A. 34:12). And the best way to give tzedakah is secretly, so the donor does not know to whom he is giving, and the poor person does not know from whom he is receiving (S.A., Yoreh De'ah, 249:7). This causes the least possible embarrassment to the person being helped.

IMITATING HASHEM THROUGH ḤESED

Tzedakah represents giving in a narrow sense—providing goods or services to assist someone who needs help. Ḥesed, however, involves much more than helping the needy. In comparing the virtues of tzedakah with those of ḥesed, the Talmud (Suk. 49b) tells us:

Rabbi Eleazar said: The practice of ḥesed is greater than tzedakah in three respects:

Tzedakah can be done only with one's money; ḥesed can be done with one's person and one's money.

This means, for example, that your presence at a time of crisis—and your sensitivity to someone else's feelings—may be more helpful than any money you could give.

Tzedakah is given only to the poor; ḥesed is given to the rich and to the poor.

This means, in part, that people who seem well-off need a kind word, a generous smile, a grateful gesture, or sincere compassion just as do the financially disadvantaged. The poor do not corner the market on misery.

Tzedakah can be given to the living only; ḥesed can be done for the living and the dead.

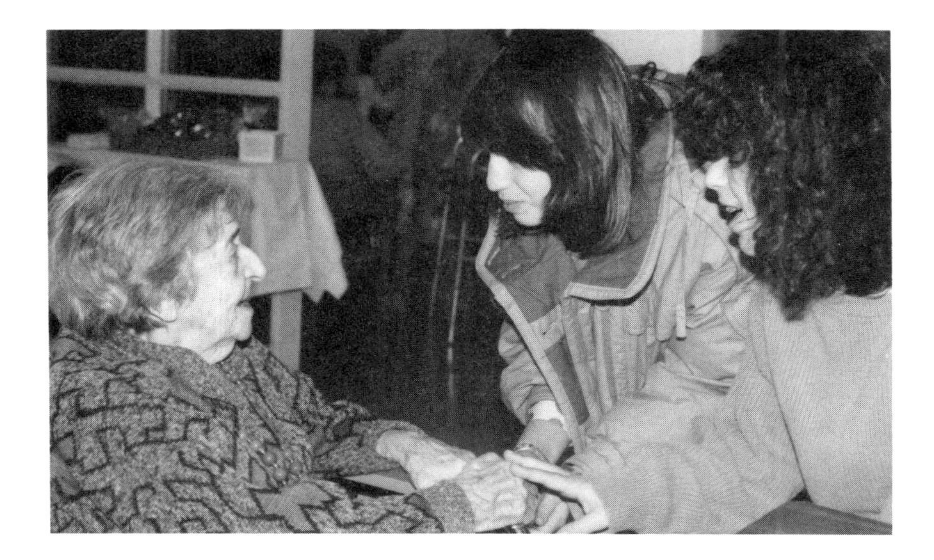

Regular visits to a Jewish home for the aging allow students to share the joys of ḥesed. A visit just before Shabbat can be especially rewarding.

Eight Levels of Tzedakah

Rambam's description in the Mishneh Torah of eight levels of tzedakah, which he based directly on the Talmud, is one of the most famous passages he wrote. The donors of tzedakah are, in ascending order of merit:

1. One who is asked and gives unwillingly.
2. One who gives less than is appropriate, but gives cheerfully.
3. One who gives a proper amount after being asked.
4. One who gives before being asked.
5. One who gives and does not know the receiver. This prevents one from displaying pity to embarrass the recipient.
6. One who gives to a known recipient, but remains anonymous to the receiver. This prevents the recipient from feeling embarrassed in the giver's presence.
7. One who gives in such a way that donor and recipient are unknown to each other.
8. One who helps a needy person to provide for himself, making future assistance unnecessary.

Examples of ḥesed for the dead include providing funds for the purchase of cemetery grounds or a funeral service, escorting the body to the grave site, comforting the mourners, and helping to support the orphans.

According to the Talmud, ḥesed is a direct imitation of HaShem. We must provide appropriate clothing for those in need, said the rabbis, because HaShem "made coats of skin for Adam and his wife, and clothed them" (Gen. 3:21). We must visit and provide for the sick because "the Lord appeared unto [Abraham] by the oaks of Mamre" (Gen 18:1), when Abraham was old and infirm. We must comfort mourners because "after the death of Abraham. . . God blessed his son Isaac" (Gen. 25:11). And we must show respect by burying the dead because "when Moses the servant of the Lord died . . . [HaShem] buried him in the valley" (Deut. 34:5-6). By imitating HaShem through acts of ḥesed, we become the people He wants us to be.

How much ḥesed you show in your everyday life reflects your most deeply held values. Consider one example: If you choose to be a physician, you study to learn all the arts of healing. When you see someone suffering, should you stop to ask who it is? Or should you do everything you can to relieve the suffering? Suppose you are a physician in wartime, and the person who is suffering is an enemy soldier. Should you still do everything you can to save him? As Jews, we can point with some pride to the way Israeli physicians have faithfully followed the principle of ḥesed by healing wounded Arab soldiers.

PIDYON SHEVUYIM

An act of ḥesed that has played a significant role in Jewish history is ransoming captives, or **pidyon shevuyim** (פִּדְיוֹן שְׁבוּיִים). According to halakhah, ransoming captives is even more important than clothing and feeding the poor.

The importance of pidyon shevuyim in itself teaches us something about Jewish history. In the time of the Mishnah, Jews—especially community leaders—were often kidnapped and held for ransom. The Mishnah required Jewish communities to try to rescue those unfortunate Jews who had fallen into evil hands.

At the same time, the Mishnah warned that "Captives should not be ransomed for more than their value, as a precaution for the general good." Debates inevitably arose over the "value" of a particular captive. Was the life of a great rabbi worth more than the life of a merchant (Git. 45a)?

A notorious kidnapping in the Middle Ages involved the great German rabbi Meir of Rothenburg, known as the **Maharam**, an acronym for **M**orenu (our teacher) **HaRa**v (the Rabbi) **M**eir. German officials abducted him and demanded an enormous ransom for his return. Knowing the Jews would suffer terrible hardship in raising this sum, the Maharam himself prohibited the Jewish community from redeeming him. He eventually died in captivity. His captors then demanded a large sum to allow his body to be buried in the Jewish cemetery. This amount was too large for most members of the community, but one very wealthy Jew agreed to pay the entire ransom provided that when he died, he could be buried beside the

The gravestones (matzevot) of the Maharam and the man who ransomed his body stand side-by-side in a German cemetery.

Visiting the Sick

These guidelines for bikkur ḥolim, found in the Shulḥan Arukh, have been adapted for modern usage:

1. It is a religious duty to visit the sick. Relatives and friends may visit the ill person at once; strangers should wait three days (it was felt that if total strangers visited at once, the patient might fear he was critically ill). If the sickness overtakes him and the person is near death, everyone may enter immediately.

2. All Jews are obliged to perform this mitzvah, not only rabbis and community leaders. The more often you visit, the more praiseworthy you become, as long as your visits do not trouble the ill person.

3. No visit fulfills the mitzvah of bikkur ḥolim without prayer. The rabbis urge us to pray in the patient's room in whatever language he knows—presumably so that the patient may understand. The tefillah need not be formal; a sincere wish for HaShem's help is sufficient. When Moses prayed for his sister Miriam, he used only five words: *El nah, refa na lah*, "Dear God, please heal her." Outside the patient's room—and preferably in the synagogue, in the presence of the Torah—we should recite the prayer in Hebrew.

4. If possible, you should avoid visiting the sick during the early morning hours, since most illnesses seem lighter in the morning. If you see the patient then, you may forgo praying for him because you think the illness is not serious or the patient has already recovered. Moreover, the early morning is a time when many doctors make their rounds and nurses begin their daily medical services; it is not a good idea to interrupt these tasks. You should also avoid visiting the sick during the last part of the day, for then the illness appears more severe than it actually is. Seeing the patient at this time might alarm you and lead you to give up hope of praying for him.

5. Where should you be in the sickroom? Preferably not too close to the patient, but also not too far; preferably at bedside, between the head and the foot of the bed. You should be on the same level as the patient, sitting rather than standing at the bedside. The patient in a hospital usually feels powerless in the face of his illness, and also because he is lying down while healthy people hover around him: nurses giving injections, doctors listening to breathing, friends and family worrying "over" him.

6. During your visit you should assist with small tasks, such as turning the patient, getting water, helping the patient to move about, filling out necessary forms, running errands, making calls, and so forth.

Maharam. Today, when visiting that cemetery, you can see two monuments side-by-side, one for the Maharam, the other for the man who ransomed him.

In recent decades, Jews have been held against their will in Syria, Ethiopia, and the Soviet Union, among other places, and Jews in free countries have helped to redeem them. Even kidnapping continues to be a problem that the Jewish community must face from time to time. And the act of pidyon shevuyim remains an act of supreme ḥesed.

BIKKUR ḤOLIM

Another act of ḥesed is visiting the sick, or **bikkur ḥolim** (בִּקּוּר חוֹלִים). If someone you know is ill, you are expected to visit that person and physically help him, pray for him, and bring him good cheer. In the Talmud, Rabbi Akiba provides an example of this mitzvah. When Rabbi Akiba heard that one of his students was ill, he went to the student's house and cleaned up his room and cheered him up. Immediately the student said to him, "You have restored me to life" (Ned. 40a).

ḤESED SHEL EMET

Generally, acts which you do in support of others—clothing the poor, feeding the hungry, and taking care of the sick, the needy, the homeless, the orphan, and the widow—all fall into the category of ḥesed. But there is an even higher level of ḥesed called **ḥesed shel emet** (חֶסֶד שֶׁל אֱמֶת), which literally means an "act of true love." The word for "true," אֱמֶת, here means "selfless." For most types of ḥesed, someone who received your kindness might someday be able to do you a kindness. But for this special, selfless kindness, you could never be repaid.

An example of ḥesed shel emet is respect for the dead, for the dead no longer have the ability to repay such kindness. When you undertake acts of ḥesed shel emet, HaShem takes special notice. People who volunteer to do the work of the **ḥevrah Kaddisha** (חֶבְרָה קַדִּישָׁא)—the "Holy Society" that helps the family of the deceased in its moment of crisis by caring for the body, cleansing and clothing it in white shrouds—are doing ḥesed shel emet. So are all those performing any act of goodness for anyone who could not possibly return the favor.

NIḤUM AVELIM

You already know how important it is to show ḥesed to someone who is ill or dying. We must visit the patient and try to lift his spirits, give him hope, listen to his concerns, and make him more comfortable. This is the mitzvah of bikkur ḥolim. When that person dies, we must help with burial needs, fulfilling the mitzvah of ḥesed shel emet.

Another important form of ḥesed, **niḥum avelim** (נִחוּם אֲבֵלִים), offers comfort to mourners. Those who most need niḥum avelim are usually the same close friends and family who helped care for the patient and then arranged for the burial. Now these mourners need to be cared for, comforted, and consoled; they need to able to speak of their loss and to gain strength from the presence of friends and loved ones. In fulfilling the mitzvah of niḥum avelim, you help the mourners overcome their grief and resume a normal life. This form of ḥesed requires forethought, sensitivity, empathy, and a good deal of self-control, because you need to focus on other people's feelings more than your own.

SHOWING CONSIDERATION FOR THE DISADVANTAGED

Judaism teaches that we should be careful about judging others. We must be absolutely certain that we are correct before we accuse someone else of doing wrong. We must use our sense of fairness, even before we use our sense of justice. We must ask before we accuse. In Avot we read: "Do not judge your friend until you are in his position."

The Prophets plead that we give special care for those who have suffered a loss—for widows and widowers, for those without families, and for the abused. We must also show raḥamim for those who suffer from mental or emotional problems.

The Torah specifically cautions us to show fairness and consideration to people with physical disabilities:

You shall not insult the deaf, or place a stumbling block before the blind. You shall fear your God: I am the Lord (Lev. 19:14).

Why does Torah speak particularly of the deaf and the blind? Because these are examples of people who cannot easily fight back when injured and who may be defrauded by bad advice. But in a

This bet knesset shows ḥesed for the deaf by allowing the whole congregation to view the Torah during the reading and by translating the text into sign language as it is read aloud.

deeper sense, we are all blind in one way or another. Not everyone is a good athlete, and very few people excel in every subject. All of us often need assistance and advice. If someone comes to you for advice and you do not give an honest answer, you are putting "a stumbling block before the blind."

SHALOM: BRINGING PEOPLE TOGETHER

The Talmud (Pe'ah 1:1) specifically lists among the very important components of ḥesed the need to bring **shalom** (שָׁלוֹם), or peace, among people. When we use the expression "Shalom" to tell someone hello or goodbye, we are really saying something like "Peace be with you." Shalom has been linked with the Hebrew word **shalvah** (שַׁלְוָה), which means 'tranquillity" or "ease."

We tend to think of shalom as making peace among nations. But before we can make peace among nations, we must bring peace to our own hearts and to people we know. We must do our utmost to prevent people from arguing and, if they do quarrel, to help them to resolve their conflict. If two of your friends have a misunderstanding, or if someone else is trying to make trouble between them, it is up to you to help repair their friendship.

In the Ḥumash, Aaron, the High Priest, is known as a peacemaker. The Midrash reports that whenever two people quarreled, Aaron would make peace between them. He would tell the first person that the second had spoken well of him, and then tell the second person that the first had done likewise. In this way, Aaron spread confidence and trust where there had been suspicion and hostility. We are bidden to be of the children of Aaron, to love peace and pursue it.

Shalom is also connected with **shalem** (שָׁלֵם), which means "whole" or "complete." From this we derive the lesson that we cannot have inner peace without a feeling of wholeness or completeness. Some people are so full of conflict that it seems as though a civil war is raging inside them. Not until they resolve their inner turmoil (perhaps by seeking professional help) can they experience the feeling of shalem that leads to shalom.

SAFETY FIRST

The Torah makes it clear that we must concern ourselves with the safety of other people. That is why it is an important positive mitzvah to build a little fence—a **ma'akeh** (מַעֲקֶה), or parapet—around the roof of a house, so anyone who goes up there will be prevented from falling (Deut. 22:8).

Many laws of ḥesed mandate safety in the things we build or use, such as fences, houses, walls, and cities. Ḥesed teaches us not to allow these to present any danger to other people. In addition, we are not permitted to keep dangerous things around the house, or in any other

One way you can practice ḥesed is by checking your home for items that might pose a hazard to young children.

place where people might find them and hurt themselves with them. In the Talmud it is said:

> How do we know that one should not keep a vicious dog or a broken ladder in his house. Because the Torah warns (Deut. 22:8): "Do not cause blood in your houses," do not do anything in your home that would cause you to be responsible for anyone's blood (B.K. 15b).

The Mishnah states that if you bury broken glass inside a stone wall to keep others from hurting themselves on the glass, you must be certain the wall will not fall. If the wall does fall, and the glass spills out, you may be held responsible for any injury the glass causes, even though you intended to protect people by hiding the glass (B.K. 3:3).

You can practice ḥesed by checking your own home for safety. Consider your sports equipment. Do you put your skates, rackets, balls, bats, nets, clubs, and other items in a safe place after you use them, a place where no one will fall over them or be hurt by them? Take a look in the medicine cabinet: the vials of unused medicines stored there may pose a potential threat. If a child visiting your house were to open the medicine cabinet out of curiosity, would the child be in danger? If so, ḥesed requires your family to conceal these medicines before something terrible happens.

Communities can practice bal tash'ḥit by recycling glass bottles, aluminum cans, newspapers, and other products. Families can practice bal tash'ḥit by planting trees and flowers.

BAL TASH'ḤIT

The principles of ḥesed require us to show kindness to people and animals. We also fulfill HaShem's purpose when we act in a kindly and caring manner toward the environment we live in. By not wasting the products of HaShem's creation, we practice **bal tash'ḥit** (בַּל תַּשְׁחִית), which literally means "do not destroy." In the Torah we read:

When in your war against a city you have to besiege it a long time in order to capture it, you must not destroy its trees with your axes. You may eat of them, but you must not cut them down (Deut. 20:19).

The sages said this prohibition applies not just to fruit trees but to anything which could be useful to other people. If someone can use a thing, you are not allowed to destroy it. The sages went on to say that you may not destroy something useful even if it belongs to you. If, in a fit of anger, you deliberately tear your clothing or smash something in your house, you are acting like an idolator who does not care about HaShem's creation (Shab. 105b). As the Shulḥan Arukh says:

Just as one must be careful not to destroy one's own body, not to impair or injure it . . . so must one be careful not to destroy, impair, or damage one's property. Whoever breaks a utensil, or tears a garment, or destroys food or drink, or filthies them, or throws money away so that it is lost, or who spoils any other thing that is fit for human enjoyment sins against the command, "You shall not waste" (Kitzur S.A. 190:3).

WORKING FOR THE COMMUNITY

A form of ḥesed you may choose as your life's work is serving the community, either through some charitable organization or through government service. Of this the Shulḥan Arukh says, "One who causes others to give tzedakah . . . his reward is greater than the reward of the donor himself . . . " (S.A., Yoreh De'ah, 249, Taz).

When you work in community service, you are often viewed with suspicion. People wonder if what you are really after is money and glory. You may be tempted to take advantage of the power and influence of the office you hold. For this reason the sages cautioned, "Let all who work for the community, work with them for the sake of heaven . . . " (Avot 2:2). Officeholders should not serve primarily for the salary or the honors, or with the thought of personal gain. Jobs in government and in community service organizations are positions of

A Dictionary of Decency

bal tash'ḥit (בַּל תַּשְׁחִית): "do not destroy"; avoidance of waste; environmental preservation.

bikkur ḥolim (בִּקּוּר חוֹלִים): the mitzvah of visiting the sick.

gemilut ḥasadim (גְּמִילוּת חֲסָדִים): benevolence; the mitzvah of showing kindness.

hakhnasat orḥim (הַכְנָסַת אוֹרְחִים): hospitality; the mitzvah of welcoming guests into your home.

ḥesed (חֶסֶד): acts of loving-kindness.

ḥesed shel emet (חֶסֶד שֶׁל אֱמֶת): an act of true (selfless) love, especially one that involves caring for the dead.

kavod (כָּבוֹד): honor; respect.

kiddush HaShem (קִדּוּשׁ הַשֵּׁם): "sanctification of the Name"; the mitzvah of glorifying HaShem through acts of piety and integrity, including martyrdom.

niḥum avelim (נִחוּם אֲבֵלִים): comforting mourners.

pidyon shevuyim (פִּדְיוֹן שְׁבוּיִים): ransoming captives.

raḥamim (רַחֲמִים): compassion.

shalom (שָׁלוֹם): peace.

sh'lom bayit (שְׁלוֹם בַּיִת): family harmony.

tzedakah (צְדָקָה): "righteousness"; the mitzvah of giving to the poor.

heavy responsibility with great influence over the lives of others. They should be approached as works of ḥesed.

In the United States, Jews have set up community institutions such as Jewish Federations to provide homes for the aged, food kitchens for those who cannot afford to feed themselves, employment agencies for those who cannot find work on their own, and so on. Every synagogue has a tzedakah fund to help people in need. Most synagogues also have special committees to visit the sick and to help widows, widowers, orphans, the homeless, and poor brides. Making donations to such charities, or working on the committees and projects they sponsor, are acts of ḥesed.

In earlier times, Jewish newcomers to America could rely on **landsmanshaften**, special societies established by previous immigrants; each landsmanshaft reflected a particular town or village of the Old Country and was set up to assist former neighbors (landsmen) from the same region. In many cases, a local group sponsored a Free Loan Society, called **Gemilat Ḥesed**, to help newcomers get started by offering them interest-free loans; many of these continue to operate to this day.

In great measure, Jews judge their community by how much benevolence, or **gemilut ḥasadim** (גְּמִילוּת חֲסָדִים), it shows. The sages felt gemilut ḥasadim was important not only to us but also to HaShem.

As Rabban Yoḥanan ben Zakkai and Rabbi Joshua were walking together in Jerusalem, they saw the ruins of the Temple. "Woe unto us," Rabbi Joshua cried, "that this place where we atoned for our sins through sacrifices is now laid waste!"

"My son," Rabban Yoḥanan replied, "be not grieved. We have another atonement as effective as this. And what is it? It is gemilut ḥasadim—as it is written (Hos. 6:6), 'For I desire goodness and not sacrifice' (ARN 4).

YOU, AND THEN OTHERS

Torah says: "You shall love your neighbor as yourself" (Lev. 19:18). This commandment can only be followed if you love yourself first. (If you do not love yourself, this law becomes very dangerous!) Judaism is not a religion which asks you to give everything you have to others. Realistically, you must first be certain you have enough for yourself.

Try to solve this puzzle, which was offered in the Talmud and Midrash (B.M. 62a; Sifra, Behar, ch. 5). Two friends are traveling through a desert. The first man has a flask of water. The second man does not. Both men walk until they are dying of thirst. If the first were to drink all the water in his flask, he might be able to reach the town at the edge of the desert, but his friend would die. On the other hand, if the men were to share the water, neither one would be able to reach the town, and both would surely die. Should the first man drink all the water? Or should he share it with his friend?

The issue is: whose life comes first when only one life may be

Jewish Community Organizations

Every Jewish community has established organizations to provide ḥesed for those in need. For example, in Los Angeles alone, more than 100 Jewish groups provide food, clothing, counseling, loans, medical care, and other services to those who need them. These groups include:

JEWISH FAMILY SERVICE— offers psychological counseling and other services for families and individuals. Special programs include Kosher Meals for the Elderly, the Community Care Facility for the Elderly, the Family Violence Project, and the Jewish Community Burial Program.

JEWISH BIG BROTHERS— pairs responsible adult male volunteers with fatherless boys and girls.

JEWISH FREE LOAN ASSOCIATION— offers interest-free loans (gemilat ḥesed) to those otherwise unable to obtain credit.

JEWISH VOCATIONAL SERVICE— provides job placement, career counseling, and vocational rehabilitation.

NATIONAL INSTITUTE FOR JEWISH HOSPICE— offers emergency counseling, publishes booklets and audiotapes, maintains a national database, and disseminates information about care for the terminally ill.

BET TZEDEK LEGAL SERVICES— provides legal representation to people who cannot afford an attorney.

CEDARS-SINAI MEDICAL CENTER— the Jewish hospital.

BUREAU OF JEWISH EDUCATION— supports affiliated Jewish schools through financial aid, curriculum supervision, and other professional services.

TOMCHEI SHABBAT— assists the needy with Shabbat meals.

Another important organization, **Hatzalah**, provides emergency medical assistance in several cities, and many communities and synagogues maintain a burial society (**Ḥevrah Kaddisha**) and a committee for bikkur ḥolim. To find out which services are available in your community, ask your rabbi or teacher, consult your local Jewish newspaper, or call the Jewish Federation office in your area.

saved? Two possible answers are given: either the first man should drink, or the two friends should share. You may ask: why not consider a third possibility? Perhaps the first man should have given all the water to the second man? Wouldn't that be the generous and righteous thing to do? It might seem so at first, but think again. If the first man was required to give the water to the second man, then the second man would become the owner of the water. By the same principle, he would then be required to give the water to the first man. At last, both men would die—as they passed the water back and forth, neither one of them drinking!

The two answers given in the Sifra both derive from the same verse, "And your brother shall live with you" (Lev. 25:36). Ben Petura answered that the two friends should share the water. He based his interpretation on the word "live," holding that both men must survive as long as they can, even though both will eventually die of thirst. Rabbi Akiba, on the other hand, said it would be better to have one dead than two. Therefore, the man who owns the water must drink it. Rabbi Akiba based his answer on "with you," interpreting these words to mean that your life takes precedence over that of your brother.

The rabbis agreed with Akiba, and they applied this principle to other real-life situations. We must think of ourselves first—though not to the exclusion of others. In many cases, if we are not strong ourselves, we cannot be of much help to others. Clearly, we must learn to love ourselves, if we are ever to learn how to love others.

The sages told the following story to help us understand the real meaning of tzedakah. From it we can also understand what it means to live a life of ḥesed, showing kindness to all.

Monobazus, a king of Adiabene, became a convert to Judaism. During a great famine in his land, he gave away all his wealth to the poor so they could buy food.

His relatives came to him and called him foolish. They complained that he was wasting their money. But Monobazus answered, "My ancestors stored up treasures for below. I have stored my treasures for above. They stored treasures in a place where force could rob them; I stored treasures where no force can harm them. They stored treasures that can bear no fruit; my treasures will be fruitful. They stored treasures of gold; I stored mine of souls. They stored up treasures for this world, but I have stored mine for the World to Come" (Tosef., Pe'ah, 4:18).

Other activities store up treasures in this world, but tzedakah stores up treasures for the World to Come. And tzedakah is just one jewel in the dazzling crown of ḥesed.

CHAPTER NINE

FAMILY

כַּבֵּד אֶת־אָבִיךָ וְאֶת־אִמֶּךָ לְמַעַן יַאֲרִכוּן יָמֶיךָ
עַל הָאֲדָמָה אֲשֶׁר־יהוה אֱלֹהֶיךָ נֹתֵן לָךְ.

Honor your father and your mother, that you may long endure on the land that the Lord your God is giving you.

(Ex. 20:12)

The first step in learning ḥesed toward all people is honoring your father and your mother. In Hebrew this is called **kibbud av va'em** (כִּבּוּד אָב וָאֵם). The Shulḥan Arukh tells us that the mitzvah of kibbud av va'em is equally binding on all—men and women, old and young. By honoring your father and mother, you learn how to honor and respect others. You learn how to honor and respect yourself. And you learn how to honor and respect HaShem.

You come into the world weak and helpless. To survive you need food, protection, bathing, diapering, clothing, and—just as important—loving. Your parents are the first and most important people in your life, committed to all these responsibilities. Your parents are the first to care for you, the first to love and teach you, the first to sacrifice their time and energy for you. Because of all that your parents do for you, HaShem commands you to give them honor:

כַּבֵּד אֶת־אָבִיךָ וְאֶת־אִמֶּךָ כַּאֲשֶׁר צִוְּךָ יהוה אֱלֹהֶיךָ לְמַעַן יַאֲרִיכֻן
יָמֶיךָ וּלְמַעַן יִיטַב לָךְ עַל הָאֲדָמָה אֲשֶׁר־יהוה אֱלֹהֶיךָ נֹתֵן לָךְ.

Honor your father and your mother as the Lord your God commanded you; so that your days may be many; and you will do well on the land which the Lord your God gives you (Deut. 5:16).

TO HONOR AND TO FEAR

At Exodus 20:12 the Fifth Commandment says:

כַּבֵּד אֶת־אָבִיךָ וְאֶת־אִמֶּךָ

Honor your father and your mother.

But at Leviticus 19:3 we read:

Yevamot 62b says: "*Bnei banim, harei kevanim*" (Behold they are like children). By this, the rabbis meant that grandparents should treat their grandchildren as though they were their own children. Similarly, you owe your grandparents the same honor and respect you owe your parents.

אִישׁ אִמּוֹ וְאָבִיו תִּירָאוּ

Each of you shall fear your mother and father.

You may notice two differences here. In the Fifth Commandment the father is named first, while in Leviticus the mother gets first mention. In Exodus 20:12, HaShem commands us to "honor" our parents; in Leviticus, however, HaShem directs us to "fear" our parents. How are we to understand the differences between these two otherwise similar mitzvot?

The Talmud explains that "honor," or **kavod** (כָּבוֹד), and "fear," or **yirah** (יִרְאָה), teach you different ways of behaving toward your parents. The different words are used to teach different actions. "Fear" means not standing in your parents' place, not taking their seats, not speaking out against what they say, and not disobeying their decisions. "Honor" means making sure they have food, drink, clothing, and a place to live, and helping them in other ways (Kid. 31b).

Why is "father" mentioned first in one mitzvah and "mother" mentioned first in the other? This, too, the Talmud explains:

[HaShem] knows that a child usually honors a mother more than a father, for she wins the child over with kindly words. For that reason [HaShem] placed

A father teaches his son the important word *ḥelek*, which means portion. Their shared portion is love of family and love for Torah.

Celebrating Shabbat together strengthens the bonds between parents and children. Traditionally, women welcome Shabbat by lighting candles and offering a silent personal prayer for the family's health and welfare.

the father first in the command to honor one's parents. [HaShem] also knows that a child usually fears a father more than a mother, because the father usually teaches the child Torah. For that reason [HaShem] placed the mother first in the command to fear one's parents (Kid. 30b-31a).

The two commandments together teach that a mother and a father should be treated equally in almost every way. Both should be honored, and both should be feared. By learning to honor and fear our parents, we learn how to honor and fear HaShem. The Hebrew word "yirah" is the closest word in the Tanakh to the English word "religion"; it means to revere, to stand in awe of, to obey, and to respect. We owe very great honor and respect to our parents, but we owe even more to HaShem.

The link between our relationship with HaShem and our relationship with our parents is emphasized by the position of the Fifth Commandment. The first four commandments (Ex. 20:2-8) deal with our relationship with HaShem, while the last five (Ex. 13-14) deal with our relationships with other people. By honoring your parents, you learn how to relate to HaShem and, through HaShem, how to relate honorably to other human beings. How you treat your family helps to determine how you will treat everyone else.

MAKING YOUR LOVE REAL

Anyone can say, "I love my mother and father." Anyone can say, "I honor my parents." Just saying "I love you," however, does not make you either loving or lovable. Showing respect and honor to parents requires caring actions as well as loving words.

The Talmud tells us about two children. One fed his father gourmet foods, while the other made his father work in a mill. Despite outward appearances, it's not hard to determine which one the rabbis regarded as the more loving son.

The father of the first child said, "Where did you get this wonderful food?" And the son answered, "Old man, eat and be quiet. Even dogs are quiet when they eat." The father of the second son worked in a mill grinding wheat. The king ordered grinders to grind wheat in the army. The son said to his father, "You come and grind wheat here, and I will go and grind wheat in the army. If the king should beat anyone for doing a bad job, let it be me and not you" (J. Pe'ah 15c).

A Yemenite Jewish scribe prepares a marriage contract, or ketubah. The ketubah must be written before the wedding and must be signed by two witnesses to the ceremony.

With this parable, the Talmud teaches that the honor you owe your parents must be reflected in every aspect of your behavior toward them. Merely giving parents fancy food or lavish gifts is not enough if you are going to treat them like dogs.

The Talmud lists some specific ways you can show your parents honor and respect:

□ Listen to their advice.

□ If they say "no," do not thoughtlessly or spitefully say "yes."

□ Call them **imma** (אִמָּה) and **abba** (אַבָּא), "mother" and "father," or "mom" and "dad," but do not call them by their given names.

□ Find ways to bring them joy and keep them from pain.

□ Always speak kindly of them to others, even though you may—deep down—disagree with them or be upset with them. Shun anyone who speaks badly of them.

□ If your father or mother has a special seat in the house, do not sit in it.

□ Never disturb your parents when they are sleeping—unless something is so very important that you think they would want to be awakened (Kid. 31b).

Similar rules of respect should hold true for a stepmother or a stepfather. You should honor them as you would your natural mother or father. They have not given you life, and yet they provide you with love, care, and protection. In your relationship with your stepparents you should follow the example of Esther and Mordecai in the Tanakh. Even though Mordecai was only Esther's uncle and guardian, she respected him as if he were her own father.

The rules for honoring both parents hold true even if your parents are divorced. You must still try with all your strength and will to honor both your father and your mother—equally. In fact, through divorce and remarriage, many children end up with more than one set of parents. The spirit of respect extends to both sets, even though this may make life extraordinarily difficult and demanding, and even in cases where the two sets of parents disagree. It is the child's duty to show respect by listening carefully to both sets of parents, and to do as much as possible of what both sets of parents want.

FROM FAMILY TO COMMUNITY

One of the most famous rabbinic stories tells of a non-Jew and the great honor he paid his mother and father. The same story is repeated by the rabbis in several places—including the Babylonian Talmud, the Jerusalem Talmud, and Deuteronomy Rabbah—to remind us how we should act toward our parents.

What does it mean to honor your father and your mother? Rabbi Eliezer the Great said: Go and see what Dama ben Netina did. His mother was a foolish person. She slapped him in front of his friends, and all he said was, "I hope that was enough for you, my mother."

Some of our sages came to Dama to buy a precious stone to replace one that was lost from the breastplate of the High Priest. The sages offered him a thousand gold pieces for the gem they wanted. Dama went into the back room and found his father sleeping; rather than disturb his father, he returned without the jewel. Thinking that what Dama really wanted was more money, the sages raised their offer to ten thousand gold pieces. When his father awakened, Dama went in and returned with the gem. Then Dama said:

"Far be it from me to make a profit from honoring my father. I will take the thousand which we first agreed upon" (J. Pe'ah 1:1f; Deut. R. 1:15).

The rabbis also taught that when you are kind to your parents—when you love, honor, fear, and obey them—your house becomes a sanctuary for HaShem.

When a person honors father and mother, the Holy One, blessed be He, says, "I see it as if I lived with them and I was honored" (Kid. 30b).

Our tradition recognizes that a child's behavior toward a parent can affect the entire community. "By the grace of children, parents win respect," the rabbis said. When children do not honor their parents, the parents are seldom honored by others in the community. But honor in the community often follows when children treat their parents with honor and respect. How we feel and the way we act toward our mothers and fathers can make a great deal of difference in their lives.

Just as you can't play a basketball game without rules and boundaries, you can't accomplish much in life without the discipline that comes from your parents and from the Jewish tradition.

EXPRESSING DISAGREEMENT

The rules the rabbis laid down for behavior toward parents are easy to state but not always easy to follow. What if a parent is mean or cruel? What if a parent is unfair, or even breaks the law? How can you love, honor, and respect a parent who acts in a way you believe is wrong? Our tradition provides guidelines for dealing with these difficult questions.

1. Never shame your parents. If you think they have done something illegal, gently remind them of the law. Don't call them liars or lawbreakers.

2. Use mercy and compassion when judging your parents. Before reaching a conclusion, try to look at the situation from their point of view.

3. If you must disagree with your parents' opinion or decision, express your disagreement politely—and, if possible, privately. Put your disagreement in the form of a question. Say it apologetically. Ask yourself if correcting them on this point is worth the pain.

This third guideline may raise a few additional questions in your mind. Perhaps you have learned in school that everyone is entitled to his or her own opinion. Why should you be required to subordinate your views to those of your parents?

The answer, in part, depends on the nature of the issues on which you disagree. Disputes regarding boyfriends, girlfriends, extra-curricular activities, curfews, and other such matters have been going on for a long time. They are a normal part of growing up. Your parents may have had similar disagreements with their parents. You need to ask yourself honestly why your parents' views differ from your own. Time teaches many lessons, some of them painful. Parents often want to prevent their children from experiencing the hurt of learning these lessons on their own.

DISCIPLINE

Parental discipline is a common source of family conflict. At times, children have reason to resent their parents. Parents interfere with children's enjoyment by not allowing them to do just as they like, by limiting their play time, by compelling them to go to school, by sending them to bed at a specified time, by saying "no" to excesses, and by setting strict rules for friendships and relationships. Later in life, children may grow to understand how parental discipline helped strengthen their bodies and their moral fiber. At the moment the limits are set, however, these future benefits may be difficult to appreciate.

An example adapted from the modern British writer G. K. Chesterton may clarify the relationship between freedom and discipline. Imagine five children standing with a football on a small plateau, about the size of a living room, atop a 5,000-foot-high mountain. Are the children running and playing? No, they are huddled together, fearful of falling off the edge. Now imagine the same plateau surrounded by a high, sturdy fence. Suddenly the children are sprinting and jumping, enthusiastically throwing the football back and forth. Why? Because they can't fall off the mountain. They are protected by the fence. The fence did not limit them. It brought them freedom!

In much the same way, your parents impose discipline in order to build a protective fence around you. At times the rules may seem overly strict, but their real purpose is to establish the limits within which you can safely grow to become a creative, contributing member of society. Discipline is necessary for many accomplishments in life, including playing a musical instrument, getting good grades, winning at sports, and developing solid friendships.

WHEN PARENTS MAKE MISTAKES

Of course, parents are only human. They sometimes make mistakes which can cause you pain. Suppose your parents order you to do something you know is wrong, something that breaks the laws of

All in the Family

These basic terms—and the sometimes fanciful explanations the rabbis offered for them—show how deeply the idea of family has influenced Jewish attitudes down through the ages.

MISHPAḤAH (מִשְׁפָּחָה): family. The word is associated with the word for language, **safah** (שָׂפָה), and it implies "people who speak the same language." People who share a common family background understand words in the same light, sensing shadings of meaning that outsiders may not grasp. At Genesis 11:6 the descendants of Noah are described as being **safah aḥat** (שָׂפָה אַחַת), of one language, and therefore of one mind (Tanḥ., Noah, 24). Another word related to mishpaḥah is **mishpaḥtiyut** (מִשְׁפַּחְתִּיּוּת), which means familiarity or intimacy.

EM (אֵם) or **IMMA** (אִמָּה): mother. The word "em" could be considered a source for three very important words in the Jewish vocabulary: **emunah** (אֱמוּנָה), faith; **emet** (אֱמֶת), truth; and **amen** (אָמֵן), "so be it," the response to a berakhah.

AV (אָב) or **ABBA** (אַבָּא): father. The consonants in אב are the first two letters of the alef-bet. This shows how essential and fundamental the father is to a child's formative years.

AḤ (אָח), **AḤOT** (אָחוֹת): brother; sister. The Hebrew word for "sewing together" is **le'aḥot** (לְאָחוֹת). This shows that brothers and sisters must help keep a family close-knit, no matter how torn it may be over one issue or another. "Aḥ" can also denote a male friend or kinsman. "Aḥot" may be applied to a female relative, companion, or sweetheart; a nurse is also called an aḥot.

Torah. Should you do exactly what your parents demand—or should you violate their wishes?

HaShem knows that we are human, that we make mistakes, that we are sometimes stubborn and wrongheaded. So the Torah has a commandment which helps you face this difficult choice, if you must. The full text of Leviticus 19:3 reads:

אִישׁ אִמּוֹ וְאָבִיו תִּירָאוּ וְאֶת־שַׁבְּתֹתַי תִּשְׁמֹרוּ אֲנִי יהוה אֱלֹהֵיכֶם.

Each of you shall fear your mother and father, and you shall keep My Sabbaths; I am the Lord your God.

While we must "fear" our parents, the passage reminds us that we must also observe Shabbat. We are not allowed to break HaShem's laws, even when parents demand that we do so. The use of the word "fear" (yirah) in the passage above tells us that while we owe very great honor and respect to our parents, we owe even more to HaShem.

OTHER FAMILY TERMS

aḥ ḥoreg (אָח חוֹרֵג): stepbrother.

aḥot ḥoreget (אָחוֹת חוֹרֶגֶת): stepsister.

av ḥoreg (אָב חוֹרֵג): stepfather.

bat dod (בַּת דּוֹד): literally, "daughter of an uncle"; a female cousin. Also **dodanit** (דּוֹדָנִית).

bat ḥoreget (בַּת חוֹרֶגֶת): stepdaughter.

ben dod (בֶּן דּוֹד): literally, "son of an uncle"; a male cousin. Also **dodan** (דּוֹדָן).

ben ḥoreg (בֵּן חוֹרֵג): stepson.

dod (דּוֹד): uncle.

doda (דּוֹדָה): aunt.

em ḥoreget (אֵם חוֹרֶגֶת): stepmother.

ḥatan (חָתָן): son-in-law; bridegroom.

ḥoten (חוֹתֵן): father-in-law. Also **ḥam** (חָם).

ḥotenet (חוֹתֶנֶת): mother-in-law. Also **ḥamot** (חָמוֹת).

kallah (כַּלָּה): daughter-in-law; bride.

saba (סָבָּא): grandpa.

savta (סָבְתָּא): grandma.

yedid (יְדִיד): friend; beloved.

yedidut (יְדִידוּת): friendship.

But that is not the end of the problem, for HaShem still requires you to honor your father and mother. The rabbis taught: When your father disobeys the words of Torah, do not say to him, "Father, you have disobeyed the words of Torah." Instead, ask him, "Father, is this what is written in the Torah?" In this way, the rabbis want us to see that parents must be treated in a kind and honorable manner at all times.

So, even when your parents ask you to break HaShem's laws, you must still be respectful toward them. You must go to them and gently explain the meaning of the law and what it requires of us. Then you must continue to love and respect your parents, following everything they say which does not go against HaShem's teachings.

At first, your parents may resent the fact that you are not following their ways. But, eventually, they may come to understand —and even accept—your commitment. After all, you are not just being stubborn or selfish. When you became thirteen (if you are a boy) or twelve (if you are a girl), you became obligated to keep the laws of HaShem.

You are following in the footsteps of your parents' ancestors, whose willingness to make the same commitment enabled the Jewish religion to survive.

COPING WITH FAMILY CONFLICT

Some young people complain that their parents never try to understand them. Perhaps you feel your parents are always criticizing you for everything you do. "Why should I keep trying to respect them," you might ask, "when they don't respect me at all?"

This question is very complicated, but some general guidelines are possible. In order to handle the problem, you need to analyze it.

1. What motivates your parents to criticize you? Are they seeking to put you down or build you up?
2. How do they criticize you? Do they offer only negatives, or do they soften the apparent negatives with positive encouragement?
3. What kinds of things do they criticize? Have you made an honest effort to examine your behavior through their eyes?
4. Is the point of difference really worth the pain of constant conflict?

It is never wrong—and in some cases it may be absolutely necessary—to seek outside help when life within your family becomes too difficult to bear. Sometimes young people are abused by stepfathers or stepmothers, uncles, aunts, cousins, brothers or sisters, or even by their own parents. Abused children cannot respect themselves for very long in such circumstances, nor can they continue to act in ways that truly honor and respect their families. Such children need help desperately, and so do their abusers. In these extreme cases, it is an act of respect to seek outside assistance from a rabbi, a teacher, your local Jewish family service, or some other professional you can talk to in confidence and security.

Even when parents act wrongly, when they do little or nothing to make you want to love them—even if they forget you entirely—you should still try to act kindly toward them. No one questions the difficulty of behaving in this manner. But honoring your parents is not something you do only because of what they do for you. It is something you do because it is the right thing to do. It is what HaShem expects you to do.

YICHUS AND FAMILY PRIDE

In Yiddish, the word **yichus**, which comes from the word for "relationship," is used to mean a worthy or distinguished family connection—a connection in which you can take pride. Having yichus might mean having as one of your ancestors a famous rabbi or scholar or a great person in any walk of life. If you come from a family with a long and interesting history, that too is a kind of yichus. The term can also be used in a negative way, as when a person with yichus uses his family's reputation or connections to gain an unfair advantage.

In general, having yichus means taking pride in the accomplishments and achievements of your family. It also encourages you to look forward to the day when people in your own family will feel they have special yichus because they are related to you. Working toward that day will give you a goal worthy of achieving. Every person, no matter how young, should think of becoming a worthy ancestor!

YICHUS AND PERSONAL ACCOMPLISHMENT

There is something more important than who your parents or your relatives are. Who are *you*?

The rabbis said: *adam karov etzel atzmo*, "A person is a relative to himself." Now this is basically a legal principle governing the rules of evidence. By the edict of Jewish law, the relatives of someone involved in a lawsuit could not give evidence in the case. If the relatives could not be witnesses, could the person who brought the

Family life means heritage, learning, love—and fun, as in this outing at a Jerusalem amusement park.

suit be his own witness? The answer was no. The law rules that a person is considered his own "relative," therefore his testimony may not be admitted into evidence.

The principle of *adam karov etzel atzmo* embodies a moral truth that shines through the law. Everyone needs self-esteem. Everyone has a legitimate concern for himself and for his own image. In order to respect others, you have to develop self-respect.

Too many people feel unworthy. Perhaps they fear they do not measure up to their parents, grandparents, siblings, or other family members. They do not recognize that they are made in the image of HaShem. These people are blessed with talents and abilities they will never fully realize. People who are self-confident, on the other hand, find it easier to relate to others and to develop their inner gifts. That is one reason why the rabbis spoke glowingly of **yichus atzmo**, "pride in your own accomplishments." As you become more resourceful, responsible, and self-confident, you provide reasons for your family to take pride in you.

BROTHERS, SISTERS, AND OTHERS

If you are an only child, you may wish you had a brother or sister at home. If you do have a brother or sister at home—or several of each—you may wish you were an only child. When you think of your brother or sister, perhaps fighting is the first thing that comes to mind. A little reflection, however, should help you recall the many good things about being siblings.

Joseph's brothers sold him into slavery, but he later forgave them and provided for them in Egypt. This illustration is by the famous nineteenth-century French artist Paul Gustave Doré.

According to the Torah, Moses' sister Miriam led the rejoicing of Jewish women at Israel's redemption.

Common sense tells us that siblings are usually more important to us than people who are not part of our immediate family. In fact, sibling relationships are usually the longest-lasting relationships we have, often beginning at the moment of birth (when you first get to meet your parents) and enduring long after your parents have passed away. Yet nowhere in the Torah does HaShem command us explicitly to honor a brother or sister. The sages derived this requirement from a single two-letter word, אֶת, which follows the word for "respect" in the Fifth Commandment and which is otherwise superfluous. The Shulḥan Arukh teaches us this lesson when it lists people (based on Leviticus 21:1-3) in whose memory we must observe the mourning period:

There are seven next of kin upon whose death one must observe the rite of mourning: Father, mother, son, daughter, brother, sister—whether from father's side or mother's side—even a married sister—wife, and husband (Based on Yoreh De'ah 372:3-4).

The Torah demonstrates how important siblings are by showing us how they act toward one another. This is not always a pretty picture. The first act of murder is committed by Cain against his brother Abel (Gen. 4). Esau is maneuvered into selling his birthright to his brother Jacob (Gen. 25). Jacob and his mother trick Isaac into giving Jacob the blessing that belongs to Esau, who then swears to kill his brother (Gen. 27). Later, Joseph is sold into slavery by his brothers (Gen. 37). In the wilderness, after the departure from Egypt, HaShem punishes Miriam and Aaron for publicly complaining against Moses, their brother (Num. 12).

By sharing sh'lom bayit with parents and siblings, we learn to seek shalom in the world at large.

But the Torah shows us the kindness as well as the cruelty in sibling relationships. Joseph's brothers and half-brothers make war against the Hivites when the prince of the Hivites rapes their sister Dinah (Gen. 34). Joseph forgives his brothers, feeds them, and makes them welcome in Egypt (Gen. 42-46). The twelve sons of Israel overcome their constant differences to remain the twelve tribes of the Jewish people, so that we trace our ancestry not only to the Patriarchs but also to the brothers. Miriam arranges for her baby brother Moses to be rescued by Pharaoh's daughter (Ex. 2:1-10). And Aaron, Moses' older brother, willingly and fearlessly serves as his younger brother's spokesman to Pharaoh and the Israelites, and keeps the people together to receive the Ten Commandments from Moses.

From these examples of kindness, loyalty, and love we learn how brothers and sisters should behave toward one another even if they don't always agree. In Chapter 5 you read about the Jewish ideal of sh'lom bayit, "family harmony." An important part of sh'lom bayit is the peace and harmony that siblings can learn to share. Since growing up in a family teaches us how to live in the world at large, sh'lom bayit is a stage in the search for shalom throughout the world.

In addition to parents and siblings, your family, or **mishpaḥah** (מִשְׁפָּחָה), includes more people who are "important others." The rabbis say that the relationship between grandparents and grandchildren can be just as close as that between parents and children. Your extended family also comprises aunts, uncles, nephews, nieces, and cousins, along with family friends who are so close you may even think of them as (and, in some cases, call them) "uncles" and "aunts." These people also deserve honor and respect.

Through your family you learn how to live in the community —how to treat others, and what kind of treatment you can expect from others. When you choose your friends, you should ask yourself, "Is this the kind of person who would be comfortable in my home, among the members of my family?" When you get older and begin to think seriously about marriage, you should ask the same kind of question about your potential marital partner. Here, too, your family serves as a way of measuring the world, helping you find your place in it.

CHAPTER TEN

AS THE SUN GOES DOWN

עַד שֶׁיָּפוּחַ הַיּוֹם וְנָסוּ הַצְּלָלִים.

As the day wanes and the shadows flee. . . .

(Song of Songs 2:17)

The sun hovers low on the horizon. Our energies are spent, and we wait impatiently for the day to end. We think of rest and comfort and companionship—of home and family. It is time for the Minḥah service. Now? But we're just tying things up, just concluding classes, just finishing the business of the day. Why is it time for Minḥah?

The Shulḥan Arukh tells us that "the reward for davening [Minḥah] is very great." Why? Because Minḥah has no landmark moment to call its own. Shaḥarit—the morning tefillah—is said before beginning the day's work. Ma'ariv—the evening tefillah—is recited after the day's work is done. But halakhah permits us to daven Minḥah at any time between just after midday and just before nightfall.

THE MEANING OF MINḤAH

The rabbis recognized that many people might find it difficult to interrupt the headlong rush of the day's business to daven Minḥah. Nevertheless, they emphasized the importance of this tefillah—and the reward for practicing it. When you make Minḥah a permanent part of your day, you gain an island of peace, a change of pace, a break from dulling details. Ramban observes that **Minḥah** (מִנְחָה) derives from the root **menuḥah** (מְנוּחָה), meaning "rest," "respite," or "stillness."

The literal meaning of "Minḥah" is "gift" or "offering." The name referred originally to the twice-a-day flour offering brought in conjunction with the sacrifice to HaShem in the Bet HaMikdash. After some time, it came to mean only the afternoon sacrifice, for which Minḥah is a substitute. Since the destruction of the Temple, the name has generally been applied only to the afternoon tefillah.

The day wanes . . . you finish your work . . . you pack up your books . . . you look forward to relaxation with friends and family. Now is the time to daven Minḥah.

Shaḥarit, Minḥah, Ma'ariv

Just as Shaḥarit, Minḥah, and Ma'ariv differ in time, setting, and mood, they also differ in the tefillot they contain.

SHAḤARIT (שַׁחֲרִית)

Birkhot HaShaḥar (בִּרְכוֹת הַשַּׁחַר): the morning berakhot, followed by portions of Torah study related to sacrifices, the rabbis' Kaddish, Psalm 30, and the mourners' Kaddish.

Pesukei D'Zimrah (פְּסוּקֵי דְזִמְרָה): psalms of praise, including the ***Ashrei*** (אַשְׁרֵי).

Borkhu (בָּרְכוּ): the invitation to daven.

Shema: with two berakhot preceding and one following.

Amidah: the Shemoneh Esreh (see Chapter 3, "The Amidah").

Taḥanun (תַּחֲנוּן): prayers for forgiveness. This section is omitted on special days.

Torah reading: on Mondays and Thursdays.

Concluding tefillot: includes Ashrei, **Uva L'Tzion** (וּבָא לְצִיּוֹן), Kaddish, Aleinu, and the **Shir Shel Yom** (שִׁיר שֶׁל יוֹם), or "psalm of the day."

We can best appreciate the special qualities of Minḥah by comparing it with the other two daily tefillot. Shaḥarit, the morning tefillah, is filled with promise. Our strength has been restored by a night of rest. The sun comes up to brighten the world, and our spirits are rich with energy and determination. We "arise like a lion," fling open the shades, and let the day flood in. Then we daven Shaḥarit with a burst of fervor.

Ma'ariv, the evening tefillah, is shrouded in darkness. As night descends, we shutter the windows, draw the blinds, lock the door, shut out the world. We master the daylight, brave and unafraid, but nighttime masters us: as we close our eyes to sleep, we lose consciousness and control. By davening Ma'ariv, we give ourselves to HaShem in faith, trusting in His protection.

Jewish tradition holds that while Shaḥarit emphasizes HaShem's benevolence, both Ma'ariv and Minḥah involve HaShem's judgment. But there is a difference between the judgment of Ma'ariv and that of Minḥah. Ma'ariv deals with **dina rafya** (דִּינָא רַפְיָא), or "soft judgment." Though the dying of the light is always a sad time, there is a redeeming feature: the Ma'ariv service assures us of the future. The Jewish day begins here, and darkness brings us the promise of light.

Minḥah, on the other hand, deals with **dina kashya** (דִּינָא קַשְׁיָא), or "harsh judgment." Minḥah is surrounded by a waning day and weakening stamina, and the future it promises is a short-lived twilight realm. Appropriately, the prayers are brief and abrupt. We begin with

MINHAH (מִנְחָה)

Ashrei: followed by the **Hatzi Kaddish** (חֲצִי קַדִּישׁ), or "half Kaddish," recited by the leader.

Amidah: the Shemoneh Esreh (see Chapter 3, "The Amidah").

Aleinu: followed by the mourners' Kaddish.

MA'ARIV (מַעֲרִיב)

Borkhu: the invitation to daven, preceded by two verses from Psalms (78:38 and 20:10) seeking pardon and forgiveness.

Shema: with two berakhot preceding and two following.

Amidah: the Shemoneh Esreh, read silently.

Aleinu: followed by the mourners' Kaddish.

the very beautiful Ashrei (Psalm 145); follow with the Amidah, so central to Jewish prayer that it is called by the generic name Tefillah; and conclude with the Aleinu, which asks HaShem to redeem the whole world. No wonder Rabbi Eliezer held that the only real petitions to HaShem come at the time of the "stillness of the sun," *dimdumei ha'ḥamah*, when the sun appears to hang motionless in the twilight sky. As the sun's rays recede, we seize the moment and raise our voices, imploring HaShem to bring us hope and deliverance.

THE PROPHECY OF ELIYAHU

The rabbis provide us with yet another important reason to daven Minḥah:

> Said Rav Ḥelbo (in the name of Rav Huna): A person should always be careful to pray the Minḥah service, for Elijah's prayer was answered only when the afternoon sacrifice was about to be offered . . . (Ber. 6b).

The First Book of Kings vividly describes how the prophet Elijah, or **Eliyahu HaNavi** (אֵלִיָּהוּ הַנָּבִיא), challenged and defeated 450 idolatrous prophets at Minḥah time. According to the Tanakh, Eretz Yisrael was parched with drought, the people were thirsting, and starvation was everywhere. The people of Israel had strayed to follow the prophets of Ba'al, whom the wicked King Ahab and his diabolical queen Jezebel had brought in from Tyre.

Because HaShem answered Eliyahu and the Israelites at Minḥah, tradition has made this tefillah the time to petition HaShem and hope for His answer. The illustration is by a seventeenth-century French artist, Charles Le Brun.

The Tanakh tells us that God sent Eliyahu to expose the prophets of Ba'al as frauds, to renew the people's faith in HaShem, and to relieve their suffering by providing rain. Eliyahu told the prophets of Ba'al to gather in the wilderness atop Mount Carmel and to choose two bullocks—one for their altar and one for his altar. They were to put no fire on either altar. HaShem would send fire to burn only one sacrifice, Eliyahu said—either theirs or his.

Masses of people gathered on the mountain. "How long will you keep hopping between two opinions?" Eliyahu demanded. "If the Lord is God, follow Him; and if Ba'al, follow him!" (I Kings 18:21). But the people did not answer.

The prophets of Ba'al then prepared their altar. From dawn to midafternoon they prayed, cried hysterically, and "gashed themselves with knives and spears . . . until the blood streamed over them" (18:28). But there was no flame on the altar. Next Eliyahu prepared his simple altar and placed the bullock on it. He dug a trench around the altar. Three times he called for water to be poured over the offering, soaking the bullock and the altar, and filling the trench with water.

When it was time for the Minḥah offering, the prophet Eliyahu came forward and said, "O Lord, God of Abraham, Isaac, and Israel! Let it be known today that You are God in Israel and that I am Your servant, and that I have done all these things at Your bidding. Answer me, O Lord, answer me, that this people may know that You, O Lord, are God; for You have turned their hearts backward."

Then fire from the Lord descended and consumed the offering, the wood, the stones, and the earth; and it licked up the water that was in the trench. When they saw this, all the people flung themselves on their faces and cried out: "The Lord alone is God! The Lord alone is God!" (18:36-39).

The rains came and the people were saved. Their impassioned outcry "The Lord alone is God!" is read to this day at the climax of **Ne'ilah** (נְעִילָה), the concluding service for Yom Kippur. Because Eliyahu and the people were answered at Minḥah, tradition has made this tefillah the time to petition HaShem and hope for His answer.

MA'ARIV AND TORAH STUDY

The set time for reciting the Shema for Ma'ariv is when three stars appear in the night sky. In some communities during summer, it is permitted "to daven Ma'ariv with the congregation immediately after Minḥah, [as close to night as possible] although it is not yet night, because of the difficulty in getting people together again" (Kitzur S.A. 70:1). When this is done, the Shema by itself is recited at home again after dark. In some congregations, time is set aside between Minḥah and Ma'ariv, during which the congregants can study Torah together.

The rabbis say, "The nights were created for the study of Torah" (Eruv. 65a). The Talmud contains a lovely lesson about studying at night:

Said Resh Lakish: He who studies the Torah at night, the Holy One, blessed be He, draws around him a string of loving-kindness [for protection]; for it is written: "By day the Lord will command His loving-kindness, and in the night His song is with me." Israel says: "For by night His song is with me." Why will the Lord command His loving-kindness by day? Because at night the song of the Torah is with Him (Ps. 42:9).

Others say in the name of Resh Lakish: He who studies the Torah in this world, which is compared to the night, the Holy One, blessed be He, will string a chord of Divine Grace around him in the world to come, which is compared to the day... (Ḥag. 12b).

Some young people resist the idea of studying at night. "I study all day," they say, "and by evening I'm very tired. I just don't have the energy to study Torah. Can't this routine wait—at least until after I'm out of school." You probably know people who always say they're too tired to do homework or study Torah after school. Strangely, they're usually not too tired to talk on the phone, watch television, play ball, or go shopping. There is usually energy aplenty. The question is—for what? One thing is clear: learning won't wait.

Hillel said: Never say "When I have time, I will study." You may never have the time (Avot 2:5).

This *kos Eliyahu*, made of red glass, dates from the early nineteenth century. Its bright color underlines its importance at the seder.

Walking, jogging, and other exercises for a strong body honor HaShem and help us make a healthy transition from the excitement of the day to the calmer pleasures of the evening.

Setting aside a time for study after the Ma'ariv service is a way of marking the transition from the hectic activities of the day to the quiet pleasures of the evening. As we direct our thoughts toward studying Torah, we turn away from the problems and conflicts of daytime. Just as running, bicycling, and walking are healthy exercises for the body, Torah study is a healthy exercise for the mind.

THE EVENING MEAL

The laws and traditions of Judaism are sometimes surprising because they seem so very modern. Concerning the evening meal, for example, the good counsel the Shulḥan Arukh offers sounds incredibly like the advice given by physicians, psychologists, and other professionals every day.

The evening meal of a normal person should be lighter than the meal one eats during the day. The benefits of this are fourfold: (1) It will preserve one's health. (2) It will avoid discomfort during the night which is caused by heavy eating [just before bedtime]. (3) One will have pleasant dreams, whereas excessive eating and drinking cause nightmares. (4) One's sleep will not be heavy, and one will be able to rise at the proper time (Kitzur S.A. 71:2).

All these benefits are as true today as when they were first recorded. Like modern scientists, the rabbis of our tradition have studied the way people act and have drawn some very solid conclusions.

Of course, you do not always have full control over the kind of dinner you eat. And there are times when you want to celebrate, and the nighttime meal is the right time for your celebration. What the

Shulḥan Arukh teaches is that you don't have to overdo it. You should learn to judge when you have had enough, and learn politely to decline food if too much is served you. That is something you can control.

APPRECIATING THE DETAILS: A CASE STUDY

Many people rush through the day and never look back. Thoughtful people review what they've done and evaluate their daily experiences. The miracles of HaShem are all around us. The tiniest details can be full of meaning if only we pay attention to them.

We can observe how much meaning the smallest details hold if we read closely the four verses of Torah (Ex. 3:1-4) that describe Moses' encounter with the burning bush.

(1) Now Moses, tending the flock of his father-in-law Jethro, the priest of Midian, drove the flock into the wilderness, and came to Horeb, the mountain of God. (2) An angel of the Lord appeared to him in a blazing fire out of a bush. He gazed, and there was a bush all aflame, yet the bush was not consumed. (3) Moses said, "I must turn aside to look at this marvelous sight; why doesn't the bush burn up?" (4) When the Lord saw that he had turned aside to look, God called to him out of the bush: ""Moses! Moses!" He answered: "Here I am."

With these four short verses, the Torah teaches lessons we can use all our lives. In verse 1, we find Moses doing everyday chores, taking care of the flock—goats or sheep—for his wife's father. He drives the flock to the mountain of Horeb, another name for Mount Sinai, the place where the Torah was later given to Moses and the people of Israel. Surely Moses' presence here cannot be accidental. From the verse, however, we cannot tell if Moses knows when he first arrives at Horeb that he is in a holy place. Like the good shepherd he is, Moses' directs his attention to the flock.

In verse 2, an "angel of the Lord" appears. In the Torah, "angels" are **malakhim** (מַלְאָכִים), or "messengers." Sometimes they appear as angels; at other times they come disguised. The malakhim who visit Abraham as he sits by the entrance to his tent come disguised as people (Gen. 18:2). The malakh that stops Abraham from sacrificing Isaac appears as an angel (Gen. 22:11). In this case, the malakh who appears before Moses comes as "a blazing fire out of a bush." HaShem is sending Moses a message, but Moses is not yet aware of it.

In verse 3, Moses notices the bush and calls it a "marvelous sight." He is curious. He asks, "Why doesn't the bush burn up?" He turns aside to look at it more closely. It is only a bush, though it seems to be aflame. Many people are so busy with their ordinary lives that they would pay little attention to such a minor detail—one bush on an entire mountain. Yet, as it happens, this is more than just a bush in flames. This is a test. HaShem wants to know whether Moses will notice it.

Birkhot Hanehenin

Judaism teaches us to acknowledge the benefits we derive from the good things HaShem has given us. The **birkhot hanehenin** (בִּרְכוֹת הַנֶּהֱנִין) and other berakhot sensitize us to the beauty and worth of the world and to the messages that HaShem constantly leaves for us. Each of the birkhot hanehenin begins with:

בָּרוּךְ אַתָּה, יהוה אֱלֹהֵינוּ, מֶלֶךְ הָעוֹלָם
"Blessed are You, Lord, our God, King of the universe. . . . "

On seeing a rainbow: זוֹכֵר הַבְּרִית וְנֶאֱמָן בִּבְרִיתוֹ, וְקַיָּם בְּמַאֲמָרוֹ, " . . . who remembers the covenant, is faithful to the covenant, and keeps the promise."

On seeing wonders of nature (lightning, high mountains, etc.): עֹשֶׂה מַעֲשֵׂה בְרֵאשִׁית, " . . . who has made the creation."

On seeing the ocean: שֶׁעָשָׂה אֶת־הַיָּם הַגָּדוֹל " . . . who has made the great sea."

On seeing beautiful trees or animals: שֶׁכָּכָה לוֹ בְּעוֹלָמוֹ, " . . . who has such as these in the world."

On seeing a person who is a Torah scholar: שֶׁחָלַק מֵחָכְמָתוֹ לִירֵאָיו, " . . . who has imparted of His wisdom to those that fear Him."

On seeing an exalted ruler: שֶׁנָּתַן מִכְּבוֹדוֹ לְבָשָׂר וָדָם, " . . . who has given of His glory to flesh and blood."

On hearing thunder: שֶׁכֹּחוֹ וּגְבוּרָתוֹ מָלֵא עוֹלָם, " . . . whose strength and might fill the world."

On hearing bad news: דַּיַּן הָאֱמֶת, " . . . the true judge."

On hearing good news: הַטּוֹב וְהַמֵּטִיב, " . . . who is good and dispenses good."

On smelling fragrant spices: בּוֹרֵא מִינֵי בְשָׂמִים, " . . . who creates diverse kinds of spices."

On smelling fragrant trees or aromatic bark: בּוֹרֵא עֲצֵי בְשָׂמִים, " . . . who creates fragrant wood."

On smelling fruits: הַנּוֹתֵן רֵיחַ טוֹב בַּפֵּרוֹת, " . . . who gives a good scent to fruit."

Surf on a beach, a gnarled old tree, a crackling bolt of lightning—all of these are reasons to bless the Creator.

In verse 4, we learn that Moses has passed the test. HaShem was waiting to see if Moses would "turn aside." Moses did. And now HaShem speaks to Moses from the lowly bush.

In some ways, HaShem's behavior seems strange. He could easily have attracted Moses' attention in some larger way. He could have appeared in a cloud of fire, in a lightning storm, in a chariot carried by cherubim. He could have called to Moses from the heavens in a voice that no one could resist. Instead, HaShem chooses to speak to Moses from a little bush. What is Torah trying to teach us?

Many lessons have been drawn from this narrative by generations of scholars and commentators. One important lesson is that HaShem constantly places messages nearby: in things that are beautiful, in things that are mysterious, in small things, in curious things. Then HaShem waits to see if we will "turn aside" as Moses did, to notice

It's fun to schmooze with a friend, as these college students are doing, but the rabbis warn us to avoid leshon hara.

the messages meant for us. The bush appears so insignificant that, in the words of the English poet Elizabeth Barrett Browning, "Only those who see, take off their shoes." If we do not see and respond to the messages HaShem leaves for us, it is only because we are not paying attention.

TAKING STOCK

According to an old Jewish belief, your soul rises to heaven to be refreshed as you sleep. Each night your soul comes to stand before HaShem. For this reason, the rabbis felt it was important for you to take stock of the day's activities before going to bed. If you find that during the day you've done something you should be ashamed of, you must ask HaShem's forgiveness; you must also ask forgiveness from those you offended. Then you should tell yourself you won't make the same mistake again.

This is the time to think about the little things you did that might have caused pain to others—even minor pain. You should try to determine how you might have hurt other people, even unintentionally, in small ways, by lying to them, mocking them, slandering them, or even flattering them. In fact, these are not small matters at all. The Torah treats with the utmost seriousness these wrongs which we commit very often, perhaps every day.

FLATTERY AND LYING

You may be surprised to hear that flattery can be hurtful, but the reason is clear enough. Flattery is a form of lying. When you flatter others, you tell them things about themselves which are untrue. You may cause them to believe that they are better than they are, or that they can do things they really can't.

The flattery might seem innocent at first. But in the end, it does no one any good—neither the flatterer nor the one who is flattered. Once you tell a lie, you often need to tell more lies to protect the first. Ultimately, a person who frequently lies cannot tell the difference between a lie and the truth. Both look the same.

Suppose you tell a friend what a nice new outfit she has on, when, in fact, you don't think the outfit looks good at all. You are trying to be nice, but instead you are being cruel. If your friend knows the truth, she learns that she can't trust you to give an honest opinion. She may even begin to think you are lying to her just to "be friends." If she doesn't know the truth, she may think the outfit looks wonderful and go out and waste her money on another just like it. She may wonder why no one else compliments her on the outfit. Then she may be terribly hurt when most of the other people she meets laugh at her outfit or whisper about how ugly it is. Similarly, if you flatter someone into thinking she is very brave, she may take risks she wouldn't ordinarily take. This may lead her to put her safety in jeopardy.

Every bride is beautiful and graceful on her wedding day, said the School of Hillel. This old photograph shows a Yemenite woman before her wedding, wearing a traditional ceremonial costume.

Of course, by needlessly criticizing someone or by offering your criticism in an insensitive manner, you can be even more cruel than by flattering falsely. The rabbis held that no one since Rabbi Akiba has equaled his ability to criticize sensitively and constructively —and he lived more than 1800 years ago! If you cannot speak without gushing flattery or criticizing harshly, it is probably better to keep silent.

In general, Jewish tradition has emphasized the need for telling the absolute truth. Menaḥem Mendel of Kotsk, a Ḥasidic rabbi who lived in nineteenth-century Poland, said that "Everything in the world can be imitated except truth, for truth that is imitated is no longer truth." Our tradition makes an exception, however, in cases where telling the strict truth might be hurtful and to no avail. So there are occasions when you may even flatter or tell a "white" lie—for example, to preserve sh'lom bayit.

The point behind this teaching is that truth, while extremely important, should not become an idol or fetish. The rabbis tell us this in the case of a bride who is not beautiful.

Our rabbis taught: How does one sing praises before a bride? The School of Shammai says: A bride just as she is.

That is, the School of Shammai urged us to tell the strict truth, not flattering her at all.

But the School of Hillel says: A beautiful and graceful bride.

Flattery on this occasion is acceptable, said the School of Hillel, since every bride is beautiful and graceful on her wedding day.

Said the School of Shammai to the School of Hillel: Supposing she was lame or blind? Is it right to say of her that she is beautiful and graceful, since the Torah says: "Keep far from falsehood"? (Ex. 23:7).

Said the School of Hillel to the School of Shammai: Consider your own words. If a man has bought an inferior thing in the marketplace, should people praise it or disparage it? Surely they should praise it. From this the sages derived the rule that a man should always conduct himself toward others in a pleasant manner (Ket. 17a).

Of course, we must always follow the rule of Exodus 23:7: "Keep far from falsehood." But there is a difference between lying and being tactful. If someone has been cheated in the marketplace, going out of your way to tell him so may cause him pain and do no one any good. Since every bride looks beautiful in the eyes of those who love her, praising her beauty on her wedding day is not really lying.

But we are not free to lie about things we know for a fact. If someone tells you the moon is made of green cheese, and you know that it isn't, you must not agree that it is. If you are unsure about the homework assignment, and a classmate calls you to ask what it is, you are not allowed to lie by saying what it might be. Even such a simple lie could cause your classmate a lot of grief.

MOCKERY AND SLANDER

When you make fun of other people, you cause them immediate embarrassment and harm. When you slander others, you hurt them by circulating false and malicious rumors behind their backs. Mockery and especially slander fall into a category of Jewish law that deals with **leshon hara** (לְשׁוֹן הָרָע), "the evil tongue." The most important work in this field in modern times was done by the saintly rabbi known as the Ḥafetz Ḥayyim, which means "he who desires life." This comes from the verse "whoever desires life . . . keep your tongue from speaking evil and your lips from deceit" (Ps. 34:13-14). It is forbidden to call someone by a derogatory name, to remind people about bad things they have done in the past, or to tell them that their problems are caused by HaShem's punishing them (Kitzur S.A. 63:2). All these things hurt others.

Jewish law takes slander very seriously. In the Torah we read: "You shall not go about spreading slander among your people; nor shall you stand by idly when your neighbor's life is at stake" (Lev. 19:16). This verse connects the sin of talebearing with the sin of murder. The rabbis said that when you hurt someone with terrible gossip, he turns pale. The draining of blood from the victim's face reminds us of the most terrible bloodletting of all—murder. The rabbis made a similar connection when they said, "What is spoken in Rome may kill in Syria" (Gen. R. 98:19).

Spreading malicious tales can divide a family or community into hostile camps. It can separate people from their families or communities just as does the punishment of exile. And it can do all

Take a quiet moment at the end of each day to review the good and bad things you've done. Have you helped bring sh'lom bayit to your family and shalom to your innermost self?

this even when there is not the slightest truth in the tales people spread. The purpose of Judaism's strong prohibition against talebearing is to keep families and communities from falling apart.

In the Book of Proverbs we read: "For lack of wood a fire goes out, and without a talebearer, strife subsides" (26:20). According to the Talmud, HaShem says, "[The slanderer] and I cannot live together in the world!" (Ar. 15b). Rambam says that talebearing is a sin even if the tale you are telling is a true one. Worst of all is the telling of tales deliberately intended to hurt someone. This is evil gossip, and the rabbis say it kills three people: the one who tells, the one who listens, and the one about whom the tale is told.

The mildest type of slander is merely saying something unkind about another person. This is **avak leshon hara** (אֲבַק לְשׁוֹן הָרָע), "the dust of evil speech" (B.B. 165a). The sages ruled that the dead as well as the living should be protected from this type of slander.

WHEN SLEEP IS NEAR

As you look back over the day, you try to remember what you've done. Was it a good day? Was it a day when people were kind to you and—more important—when you were kind to others? Did you leave a lot of business unfinished?

Do you feel peaceful when you think back on the day? This is really the main question. Just as you try to bring sh'lom bayit to your family and home, you should try to bring shalom into your innermost self. Before you settle down to sleep, it is good to think for a short while about how well you are doing at the task of making your self more shalem—wholesome—in order to achieve shalom—inner peace.

After you have looked at what you may have done to others, think for a moment about what others may have done to you. The Shulḥan Arukh has some suggestions to help you do this. Try to forgive anyone who has caused you pain during the day, so that no one will be punished on your account. Say "I forgive anyone who has annoyed me." Next list the people by saying, "Creator of the universe, I forgive [name]." Then the business of the day can be put behind you and forgotten.

Before sleep, there is time for one last prayer asking HaShem to protect us while we are unable to protect ourselves. Recite the first section of the Shema—the Shema and the V'Ahavta. If you have not said the Shema after dark, you should recite the entire Shema at bedtime.

The Shulḥan Arukh says that sleep can be like a mitzvah. If you concentrate before you go to sleep, and you determine that the purpose of rest is to help you regain your strength so you can better serve HaShem, then He counts your sleep as an act of **avodat HaShem** (עֲבוֹדַת הַשֵּׁם), service to HaShem (Kitzur S.A. 71:4).

Before you close your eyes, take one last look around you. The world is a wonderful place. Each day is a treasure. Many people forget this. They remember to complain and to cry, but they forget to love and laugh and enjoy. Complaining and crying do not help them, and forgetting to love and laugh and enjoy can really hurt them.

Derekh hatov, the path to goodness, begins with the recognition that the world is both a gift and a blessing. It is your world. It is the best of all worlds, but it is also a world that you can help make even better. It is a place where you can discover HaShem and the good that is in today and tomorrow.

EPILOGUE

THE GOOD WEEK

My purpose in this book has been to show how we can sanctify the weekday and transform the commonplace into an uncommon experience. In our study of the Jewish approach to shavu'a tov—a good week—we have relied on the Shulḥan Arukh for guidance. Many books have been written on Judaism throughout the centuries, but very few of them have had as much influence as the Shulḥan Arukh. It is so richly meaningful that you could spend years studying it and still feel you had barely scratched the surface.

SUMMING UP

Nevertheless, we have covered a lot of ground together. We have spoken of the daily life of the Jew, from the time we rise up in the morning to the time we go to sleep. And we have spoken about the normal kinds of things that happen in that space of time. We have acknowledged that life isn't always routine. Sometimes there are surprises—some of them pleasant, some of them very difficult to bear. This is the life of the Jew.

In seeking the way to shavu'a tov, we have learned several important lessons.

- The Jewish way of life is dedicated to serving HaShem, who created our world and who sets the pattern for our lives.
- The Jewish way of life is rooted in the study of Torah.
- The Jewish way of life is committed to ḥesed as the fulfillment of our creation in the image of HaShem.
- The Jewish way of life is devoted to making daily life kadosh through study, ḥesed, tefillah, and other mitzvot.
- The Jewish way of life impresses upon us the need for shalom in our families, our communities, and our world.
- The Jewish way of life teaches us that all of Creation is the subject of Torah, because everything was created by HaShem for our use.

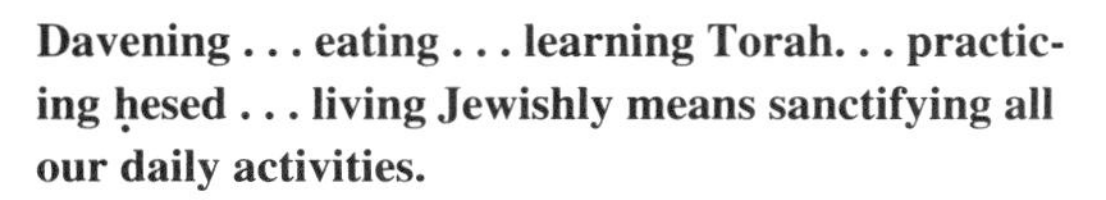

Davening . . . eating . . . learning Torah. . . practicing ḥesed . . . living Jewishly means sanctifying all our daily activities.

REMEMBERING HASHEM

The rabbis said bringing kedushah into your life depends on one short verse from the Tanakh: "In all you do you must consider God" (Prov. 3:6). Whether you are working or resting, talking or listening, walking or sitting, rising up or lying down, you should bear in mind your relationship with HaShem and your responsibility to the Jewish heritage and tradition.

Throughout this book I have tried to uncover the ways we may "consider" HaShem—at home, in school, at work, at prayer. In exploring how Judaism shapes and enriches our daily lives, I hope you have deepened your full-time commitment to make every week shavu'a tov.

SOURCES
CITED IN THE TEXT

Entries are organized alphabetically by title, followed by the abbreviation and a brief description or publication data. Unless otherwise indicated, talmudic citations apply to the Babylonian Talmud; citations to the Jerusalem Talmud are indicated by a "J." before the name of the tractate.

Arakhin (Ar.):"Valuations"; tractate of the Talmud.
Avodah Zarah (A.Z.): "Idol Worship"; tractate of the Talmud.
Avot: "Ancestors"; tractate of the Talmud.
Avot de Rabbi Nathan (ARN): "The Ancestors According to Rabbi Nathan"; talmudic text generally printed at the end of the fourth division, Nezikin ("Torts").
Bava Batra (B.B.): "Last Gate"; tractate of the Talmud.
Bava Kamma (B.K.): "First Gate"; tractate of the Talmud.
Bava Metzi'a (B.M.): "Middle Gate"; tractate of the Talmud.
Berakhot (Ber.): "Blessings"; tractate of the Talmud.
Deuteronomy (Deut.): fifth book of Ḥumash; Devarim.
Deuteronomy Rabbah (Deut. R.): midrashic commentary on the Book of Deuteronomy.
Ecclesiastes Rabbah (Eccl. R.): midrashic commentary on the Book of Ecclesiastes (Kohelet).
Eruvin (Eruv.): "Boundaries"; tractate of the Talmud.
Exodus (Ex.): second book of Ḥumash; Sh'mot.
Exodus Rabbah (Ex. R.): midrashic commentary on the Book of Exodus.
Genesis (Gen.): first book of Ḥumash; Bereshit.
Genesis Rabbah (Gen. R.): midrashic commentary of the Book of Genesis.
Gittin (Git.): "Divorces"; tractate of the Talmud.
Ḥagigah (Ḥag.): "Festival"; tractate of the Talmud.
Halakhic Man. By Joseph B. Soloveitchik. Philadelphia: Jewish Publication Society of America, 1983.
Hosea (Hos.): book of the Tanakh (Nevi'im).
Joshua (Josh.): book of the Tanakh (Nevi'im).
Ketubot (Ket.): "Marriage Contracts"; tractate of the Talmud.
Kiddushin (Kid.): "Betrothal"; tractate of the Talmud.
Kings: two books of the Tanakh (Nevi'im), divided into I and II; along with Joshua, Judges, and I and II Samuel, known as Nevi'im Rishonim ("Former Prophets").

Kitzur Shulḥan Arukh (Kitzur S.A.): condensed version of the Shulḥan Arukh, by Rabbi Solomon Ganzfried.
Kol Bo: "Everything Within"; halakhic work written around 1300 C.E.
Kuzari: "Khazars"; a philosophical work by Judah HaLevi.
The Laws of Berachos. By Binyamin Forst and Aaron D. Twerski. New York: Artscroll Mesorah, 1990.
Leviticus (Lev.): third book of Ḥumash; Vayikra.
Mekhilta: midrashic commentary on the Book of Exodus.
Menaḥot (Men.): "Meal Offerings"; tractate of the Talmud.
Mishneh Torah (M.T.): "Codification of the Torah"; law code by Moses Maimonides, or Rambam.
Nedarim (Ned.): "Vows"; tractate of the Talmud.
Niddah (Nid.): "Menstruation"; tractate of the Talmud.
Numbers (Num.): fourth book of Ḥumash; Bemidbar.
Numbers Rabbah (Num. R.): midrashic commentary on the Book of Numbers.
Pe'ah: "Corner"; tractate of the Mishnah.
Pesaḥim (Pes.): "Laws of Passover"; tractate of the Talmud.
Proverbs (Prov.): book of the Tanakh (Ketuvim); Mishlei.
Psalms (Ps.): book of the Tanakh (Ketuvim); Tehillim.
The Sabbath: A Guide to Its Understanding and Observance. By Dayan Dr. I. Grunfeld. London: Sabbath League of Great Britain, 1954.
Sanhedrin (Sanh.): "Court of Justice"; tractate of the Talmud.
Shabbat (Shab.): "Sabbath"; tractate of the Talmud.
ShaKh: acronym for *Siftei Kohen*; commentary on the Shulḥan Arukh by Shabbetai ben Meir HaKohen.
Shulḥan Arukh (S.A.): "Prepared Table"; law code by Joseph Karo.
Sifra: midrashic commentary on the Book of Leviticus.
Sifrei Deuteronomy (Sif. Deut.): midrashic commentary on the Book of Deuteronomy.
Sukkah (Suk.): tractate of the Talmud.
Tanḥuma (Tanḥ.): midrashic commentary on the Ḥumash.
Tosefta (Tosef.): "Addition"; collection of halakhot added to the Mishnah.
Yoma: "The Day"; tractate of the Talmud.

GLOSSARY

Akiba (c. 50-135 C.E.), outstanding rabbi of the mishnaic period.

Amidah (עֲמִידָה), literally, "standing"; the heart of every formal Jewish religious service, including Shaḥarit, Minḥah, and Ma'ariv. *See also* **Shemoneh Esreh; tefillah**.

Avodah (עֲבוֹדָה), literally, "worship." 1. The ancient Temple service. 2. A blessing in the Amidah which calls for the restoration of the Temple in Jerusalem.

bal tash'ḥit (בַּל תַּשְׁחִית), literally, "do not destroy." 1. The sin of waste. 2. The mitzvah of environmental preservation.

berakhah (בְּרָכָה), *pl.* **berakhot** (בְּרָכוֹת), blessing; benediction. *See also* **Birkat HaMazon, birkhot hamitzvot, birkhot hanehenin**.

Bet HaMikdash (בֵּית הַמִּקְדָּשׁ), either of the two ancient temples in Jerusalem.

bet knesset (בֵּית כְּנֶסֶת), literally, "meeting house"; the synagogue.

bet midrash (בֵּית מִדְרָשׁ), literally, "house of study." 1. A place for the study of Torah and Talmud. 2. A yeshiva.

Bet Ya'akov (בֵּית יַעֲקֹב), literally, "House of Jacob"; the Jewish people.

Bet Yisrael (בֵּית יִשְׂרָאֵל), literally, "House of Israel"; the Jewish people.

bikkur ḥolim (בִּקּוּר חוֹלִים): the mitzvah of visiting the sick.

Birkat HaMazon (בִּרְכַּת הַמָּזוֹן), "Grace after Meals"; berakhot of thanksgiving, said after every meal that includes bread.

birkhot hamitzvot (בִּרְכוֹת הַמִּצְוֹת), berakhot recited before performing a mitzvah.

birkhot hanehenin (בִּרְכוֹת הַנֶּהֱנִין), berakhot that bless HaShem for enabling us to enjoy the wonders of His creation.

davening, praying. From the Yiddish word **daven**, which is based on the French *devant*, meaning "before."

derekh eretz (דֶּרֶךְ אֶרֶץ), literally, "the way of the land." 1. Proper behavior. 2. Manners. 3. An occupation or livelihood. 4. Secular culture.

derekh hatov (דֶּרֶךְ הַטּוֹב), the good way; the path to goodness.

d'var Torah (דְּבַר תּוֹרָה), words of Torah, to be spoken at every meal.

Eretz Yisrael (אֶרֶץ יִשְׂרָאֵל), the land of Israel.

Gemara (גְּמָרָא), from the Aramaic root meaning "learning." 1. Rabbinic discussions of the Mishnah, recorded between 200 and 500 C.E. 2. The entire Talmud. *See also* **Torah sheb'al peh**.

gemilut ḥasadim (גְּמִילוּת חֲסָדִים), the mitzvah of generosity or benevolence.

genevat da'at (גְּנֵיבַת דַּעַת), deception.

hakhnasat orḥim (הַכְנָסַת אוֹרְחִים), literally, "welcoming visitors"; the mitzvah of hospitality.

halakhah (הֲלָכָה), *pl.* **halakhot** (הֲלָכוֹת). 1. The body of Jewish law. 2. A particular law or regulation.

HaShem (הַשֵּׁם); literally, "the name"; a substitute designation for the name "God."

Havdalah (הַבְדָּלָה), literally, "separation"; the ceremony separating Shabbat and Yom Tov from the rest of the week.

ḥesed (חֶסֶד), the mitzvah of showing kindness and consideration.

ḥesed shel emet (חֶסֶד שֶׁל אֱמֶת), an act of selflessness or true love, especially one that involves caring for the dead.

ḥukkat hagoy (חֻקַּת הַגּוֹי), literally, "law of the nations"; customs and practices that Jews are forbidden to adopt.

Ḥumash (חוּמָשׁ), from the Hebrew word for "five"; the first of the three main sections of the Tanakh; the first five books of the Hebrew Bible; also called **Torah**.

Kaddish (קַדִּישׁ), literally, "sanctification"; a prose poem glorifying HaShem that is recited in memory of the dead.

kadosh (קָדוֹשׁ), literally, "set apart"; holy.

kasher (כָּשֵׁר), proper; fit to eat.

kashrut (כַּשְׁרוּת), literally, "fitness"; the Jewish dietary laws.

kavanah (כַּוָּנָה), intensity, devotion, or concentration, especially in prayer.

kavod (כָּבוֹד), honor; respect.

kedushah (קְדֻשָּׁה). 1. Holiness. 2. The central prayer of the Amidah.

Ketuvim (כְּתוּבִים), "Writings"; the last of the three main sections of the Tanakh, including Psalms, Proverbs, and other books.

kibbud av va'em (כִּבּוּד אָב וָאֵם), the mitzvah of honoring your father and mother.

kiddush HaShem (קִדּוּשׁ הַשֵּׁם), literally, "sanctification of the Name"; the mitzvah of glorifying HaShem through public acts of piety and integrity, including martyrdom.

kippah (כִּפָּה), skullcap, popularly called a yarmulke.

klaf (קְלָף). 1. The piece of parchment inside a mezuzah, on which are written two paragraphs of the Shema. 2. The hide of a kosher animal.

kohen (כֹּהֵן), *pl.* **kohanim** (כֹּהֲנִים), priest.

korban (קָרְבָּן), *pl.* **korbanot** (קָרְבָּנוֹת), animal sacrifice offered at the Temple in Jerusalem.

leshon hara (לְשׁוֹן הָרָע), literally, "the evil tongue"; slander; gossip.

Ma'ariv (מַעֲרִיב), the evening tefillah.

mezuzah (מְזוּזָה) *pl.* **mezuzot** (מְזוּזוֹת), literally, "doorpost"; a small parchment scroll, enclosed in a case or shell, affixed to an outside doorpost and to the doorposts of most rooms in the house, including the kitchen, living room, dining room, and bedrooms.

midrash (מִדְרָשׁ), literally, "investigation." 1. A rabbinic explanation of a passage in the Tanakh; some midrashim articulate a point of halakhah, others a moral maxim. 2. *cap*. The whole of midrashic literature.

Minḥah (מִנְחָה), literally, "gift" or "offering"; the afternoon tefillah.

minyan (מִנְיָן), a quorum of ten men; the minimal requirement for congregational worship and for the recitation of certain prayers.

Mishnah (מִשְׁנָה), from the Hebrew word meaning "to repeat" or "to teach"; code of Jewish law compiled around 200 C.E. by Rabbi Judah HaNasi. *See also* **Gemara; Talmud; Torah sheb'al peh**.

Mishneh Torah (מִשְׁנֵה תּוֹרָה), law code compiled by Rambam.

mishpaḥah (מִשְׁפָּחָה), family.

mitzvah (מִצְוָה), *pl.* **mitzvot** (מִצְוֹת), literally, "commandment"; an action required by HaShem.

Musaf (מוּסָף), additional tefillah; the service recited on Shabbat, festivals, and the new moon.

nevelah (נְבֵלָה), food that comes from an animal that was not slaughtered according to the laws of kashrut.

Nevi'im (נְבִיאִים), "Prophets"; the second of the three sections of the Tanakh.

niḥum avelim (נִחוּם אֲבֵלִים), the mitzvah of comforting mourners.

penimah (פְּנִימָה), literally, "interior"; inner self.

pesukei d'zimrah (פְּסוּקֵי דְזִמְרָה), literally, "songs of praise"; psalms recited before Shaḥarit.

pidyon shevuyim (פִּדְיוֹן שְׁבוּיִים), the mitzvah of ransoming captives.

pushka, a charity box.

raḥamim (רַחֲמִים), from **reḥem** (רֶחֶם) , "womb"; compassion.

Rambam, acronym for the great Jewish scholar and physician **Ra**bbi **M**oshe **b**en **M**aimon, also known as Moses Maimonides (1135-1204); he lived in Spain and North Africa. *See also* **Mishneh Torah**.

Ramban, acronym for the outstanding Spanish Jewish scholar and philosopher **Ra**bbi **M**oshe **b**en **N**aḥman, also known as Naḥmanides (1194-1270).

Rashi, acronym for the famous French Jewish commentator on Ḥumash, **Ra**bbi **Sh**lomo ben **I**saac (1040-1105).

responsa, rabbinic answers to questions and problems submitted by Jewish communities through the ages; known in Hebrew as שְׁאֵלוֹת וּתְשׁוּבוֹת.

sefer Torah (סֵפֶר תּוֹרָה), the Torah scroll.

Shabbat (שַׁבָּת), from the Hebrew word meaning "to rest"; the Jewish sabbath.

Shaḥarit (שַׁחֲרִית), the morning tefillah.

shalom (שָׁלוֹם), peace.

SHAS (ש"ס), acronym for **Shishah Sedarim** (שִׁשָּׁה סְדָרִים), "Six Orders [of the Mishnah]"; the Talmud.

shavu'a tov (שָׁבוּעַ טוֹב), "a good week'; a traditional greeting at Havdalah, which marks the beginning of the Jewish week.

sheḥitah (שְׁחִיטָה), kosher slaughter.

Shema (שְׁמַע), literally, "hear." 1. The central statement of Jewish belief, affirming in six Hebrew words the essential oneness of HaShem. 2. The three-paragraph prayer that begins with those words.

Shemoneh Esreh (שְׁמוֹנֶה עֶשְׂרֵה), literally, "eighteen"; the series of blessings, now nineteen in all, that constitutes the weekday Amidah.

sh'lom bayit (שְׁלוֹם בַּיִת), literally, "peace in the house"; family harmony.

shoḥet (שׁוֹחֵט), a person qualified to perform kosher slaughter.

Shulḥan Arukh (שֻׁלְחָן עָרוּךְ), literally, "Prepared Table"; essential code of Jewish law, compiled in the sixteenth century in Safed by Rabbi Joseph Karo.

siddur (סִדּוּר), literally, "order"; the Jewish prayer book.

sofer (סוֹפֵר), a scribe.

tallit (טַלִּית), prayer shawl.

tallit katan (טַלִּית קָטָן), literally, "small tallit"; a square cloth, with fringes at each corner, worn by Jewish men and boys under their shirts.

Talmud (תַּלְמוּד), literally, "learning" or "instruction"; document of the central halakhic principles and traditions of the Jewish people, compiled by 500 C.E. Talmud consists of Mishnah and Gemara, a term sometimes applied to the entire Talmud. *See also* **Torah sheb'al peh**.

Tanakh (תַּנַ"ךְ), acronym for Torah, Nevi'im, Ketuvim; the Hebrew Bible, consisting of Ḥumash, the Prophets, and other writings.

tefillah (תְּפִלָּה), *pl.* **tefillot** (תְּפִלּוֹת). 1. A prayer. 2. A worship service. 3. *cap.* The Amidah.

tefillah b'tzibbur (תְּפִלָּה בְּצִבּוּר), public worship, for which a minyan is required.

tefillat shav (תְּפִלַּת שָׁוְא), a useless prayer.

tefillat yahid (תְּפִלַּת יָחִיד), private or individual worship.

tefillin (תְּפִלִּין), "phylacteries"; leather straps attached to two small leather boxes (batim) that contain paragraphs from the Torah; one of the batim is worn on the arm, the other on the head.

terefah (טְרֵפָה), literally, an animal torn by a wild beast; any food ritually unfit to be eaten. *See also* **nevelah**.

Torah (תּוֹרָה), literally, "guidance" or "instruction." 1. Halakhah. 2. The Ḥumash. 3. The sacred writings of the Jewish people. 4. The entire body of Jewish religious knowledge.

Torah lishmah (תּוֹרָה לִשְׁמָהּ), Torah for its own sake.

Torah sheb'al peh (תּוֹרָה שֶׁבְּעַל פֶּה), the Spoken Torah, explanations and elaborations of the Written Torah, eventually compiled in the Talmud.

Torah shebikhtav (תּוֹרָה שֶׁבִּכְתָב), the Written Torah, a term used to describe the Ḥumash and, often, the Nevi'im and Ketuvim as well.

tractate, a principal book of the Mishnah or Talmud.

tzedakah (צְדָקָה), literally, "righteousness"; the mitzvah of giving to others.

tzitzit (צִיצִית), literally, "fringes." 1. The fringes of the tallit. 2. The tallit katan.

tzni'ut (צְנִיעוּת), modesty (in dress); sexual integrity.

yichus, from the Yiddish word for "relationship"; a worthy or distinguished family connection.

yirah (יִרְאָה), fear; awe; piety; respect.

yirat shamayim (יִרְאַת שָׁמַיִם), "fear of heaven"; reverence for HaShem.

Yom Tov (יוֹם טוֹב), literally, "good day"; a holiday with specific halakhic requirements.

INDEX

OF SUBJECTS DISCUSSED IN THE TEXT

PHOTO CREDITS

The editors and publisher gratefully acknowledge the cooperation of the following sources of photographs for this book:

In the text: Janet Abramowitz on behalf of Yeshivat Rambam, Baltimore, 133; A.I.C.F., 166; Bill Aron, 3 (courtesy of Jack Roth Booksellers), 5 (bottom), 10, 13 (courtesy of Jack Roth Booksellers), 14, 19 (both photos), 20, 23, 26, 27, 28 (right), 32, 35 (right), 37, 41, 43, 46, 50, 51, 53 (bottom), 54, 59, 60, 65, 67, 71 (bottom), 74, 78 (top), 79, 82, 83, 85 (top), 86-87, 89, 91 (bottom), 93, 96, 98, 99, 102, 103 (top left), 105 (top), 109, 111, 113 (top), 121 (bottom), 130, 144, 155, 163 (left), 171 (all except top right); Bettmann Archive, 63 (Reuters/Bettmann), 71 (top), 91 (top); Black Star, 35 (left; Jim Nachtwey); FPG International, 68 (Carolyn A. McKeone), 121 (top; R. Nowitz), 133 (Jeffrey Sylvester), 140 (Nowitz), 142 (Isaiah Karlinsky), 160 (John Terence Turner), 163 (right; Bill Porta), 171 (top right); Globe Photos, 15 (Rick Shinabery), 114 (Roy Pinney), 118 (Pinney), 132 (Bill Greenslade); Historical Pictures Service, 150, 151, 158; Jewish Museum, 77 (Frank J. Darmstaedter), 78 (bottom), 159; Jewish Theological Seminary of America, ii (Darmstaedter); Magnum, 5 (top), 30 (Cornell Capa), 36 (Ian Berry), 105 (bottom; Leonard Freed and Gilles Peress), 141 (Freed); Keren Hayesod, 110; Shirley Lamm, 127; Manhattan Day School/Rebecca Zweibon, 28 (left), 85 (bottom); Photo Researchers, 53 (top; Katrina Thomas), 100 (Michael C. Hayman), 107 (Aron), 116 (Abraham Menashe), 139 (David M. Grossman), 162 (Fritz Henle), 164 (Barbara Rios), 168 (Chester Higgins, Jr.); S.A.R. Academy/Devorah Preiss, 21, 94, 123, 125; Superstock, 66, 152; Sygma, 16 (Alain Keler), 47 (William Karel), 149 (Karel); Zionist Archives and Library, 108. On the cover: © Earth Imaging.